The Brookes
Transition to
Adulthood Series

PLANNING THE
Transition to Employment

The Brookes
Transition to
Adulthood Series

PLANNING THE
Transition to
Employment

Wendy S. Parent-Johnson, Ph.D., CRC, CESP
University of Arizona
Tucson, AZ

Laura A. Owens, Ph.D., CESP
University of Wisconsin-Milwaukee
Milwaukee, WI

Richard Parent-Johnson, Ph.D.
University of Kansas
Lawrence, KS

·P·A·U·L·H·
BROOKES
PUBLISHING Cº ®

Baltimore • London • Sydney

Paul H. Brookes Publishing Co.
Post Office Box 10624
Baltimore, Maryland 21285-0624
USA

www.brookespublishing.com

Typeset by Progressive Publishing Services, York, Pennsylvania.
Manufactured in the United States of America by Sheridan Books, Inc., Chelsea, Michigan.

The individuals described in this book are composites or real people whose situations are masked and are based on the authors' experiences. In all instances, names and identifying details have been changed to protect confidentiality.

Library of Congress Cataloging-in-Publication Data

Names: Parent-Johnson, Wendy S., author. | Owens, Laura A., 1961– author. | Parent-Johnson, Richard, author.
Title: Planning the transition to employment / by Wendy S. Parent-Johnson, Ph.D., CRC, CESP, University of Arizona, Tucson, AZ; Laura A. Owens, Ph.D., CESP, University of Wisconsin-Milwaukee, Milwaukee, WI; and Richard Parent-Johnson, Ph.D., University of Kansas, Lawrence, KS.
Description: Baltimore : Paul H. Brookes Publishing Co., [2020] | Series: Brookes transition to adulthood | Includes bibliographical references and index.
Identifiers: LCCN 2019007911 (print) | ISBN 9781598573589 (pbk. : alk. paper)
Subjects: LCSH: Youth with disabilities–Education (Secondary)–United States. | Youth with disabilities–Vocational guidance–United States. | Youth with disabilities–Employment–United States. | School-to-work transition–United States.
Classification: LCC LC3981 .P37 2020 (print) | LCC LC3981 (ebook) | DDC 371.9/0473–dc23
LC record available at https://lccn.loc.gov/2019007911
LC ebook record available at https://lccn.loc.gov/2019980075

British Library Cataloguing in Publication data are available from the British Library.

2023   2022   2021   2020   2019

10   9   8   7   6   5   4   3   2   1

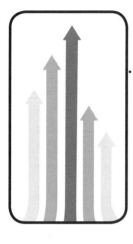

Contents

Series Preface vii
Editorial Advisory Board ix
About the Authors xi
Preface xiii
About the Downloads xv
Acknowledgments xvii

1   Getting Started 1
    Transition to Employment 1
    Importance of Work 2
    What Do the Statistics Say? 2
    Changing the Landscape of Disability
        and Employment 3
    Upcoming Chapters 5

2   Strategies to Facilitate Effective Transitions 7
    Teacher Vignette 7
    The Crucial Importance of Collaboration 8
    Grow Your Own Collective Impact Team 10
    Collective Impact: A Practical Application 11
    Integrating Best Practices 17

3   Planning for Employment: Person-Centered
        Planning and Adult Agency Involvement 27
    Teacher/Transition Coordinator Vignette 27
    Planning for Employment 29
    Ready and Reliable 30
    Employment First 33
    Why Is Person-Centered Planning Important? 34

4   Developing Skills, Identifying Passions,
    and Exploring Careers 47
    Teacher/Transition Coordinator Vignette 47
    Developing High School Services 48
    Identifying Learning Styles and Preferences 51
    Utilizing Online Career Exploration Tools 54
    Providing Community Work and Internship
    Opportunities 61
    Establishing Employment or
    Postsecondary Education Areas of Interest 63

5   Developing Employer Relationships
    to Create Job Opportunities 67
    Teacher/Transition Coordinator Vignette 67
    Competitive Integrated Employment 67
    Knowing the Business Community 68
    Business Knowledge 69
    Networking 70
    Meeting With Employers 74
    Employment Proposals 77
    Preparing Students for Employment Through
    Work-Based Learning or Internships 77
    Partnership Agreement 80
    Worksite Analysis 80
    Intern Criteria and Job Description 80
    Application and Interview Process 80
    Orientation and Training 83
    Evaluation Process 83

6   Providing Training and Supports While in
    School and After 91
    Teacher/Transition Coordinator Vignette 91
    Teaching Self-Determination 92
    Identifying Instructional Strategies and
    Support 93
    Instructional Strategies 93
    Natural Supports 95

7   Ways to Overcome the *Yeah, but* . . . Syndrome 107
    Student Vignette 107
    Case Studies 109
    Challenges That Teachers Face 117
    Pulling It All Together 119

References 121
Index 125

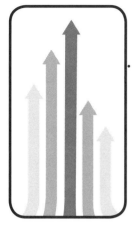

Series Preface

The Brookes Transition to Adulthood Series was developed for the purpose of meeting the critical educational needs of students with disabilities who will be moving from school to adulthood. It is no longer acceptable to simply equip a student with a set of isolated life skills that may or may not be relevant to his or her adult life. Nor is it sufficient to treat the student as if he or she will remain unchanged throughout life. As we allow for growth and change in real-life environments, so must we allow for growth and change in the individuals who will operate within the environments. Today, transition must concern itself with the whole life pattern of each student as it relates to his or her future. However, integrating the two constructs of self and the real adult world for one student at a time is not always straightforward. It requires skills and knowledge. It requires a well-thought-out, well-orchestrated team effort. It takes individualization, ingenuity, perseverance, and more.

The results of these first-rate efforts can be seen when they culminate in a student with a disability who exits school prepared to move to his or her life beyond the classroom. Unfortunately, though, this does not always happen. This is because transition has become a splintered concept, too weighted down by process and removed from building on the student's aspirations and desires for a good life. However, it does not have to be this way.

This book series is designed to help the teachers, transition specialists, rehabilitation counselors, community service providers, administrators, policy makers, other professionals, and families who are looking for useful information on a daily basis by translating the evidence-based transition research into practice. Each volume addresses specific objectives that are related to the all-important and overarching goal of helping students meet the demands of school and society and gain a greater understanding of themselves so that they are equipped for success in the adult world.

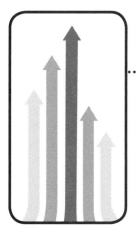

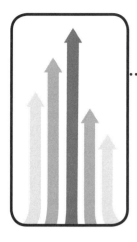

About the Authors

Wendy Parent-Johnson, Ph.D., CRC, CESP
Sonoran UCEDD
University of Arizona
Department of Family & Community Medicine
1521 E. Helen Street
Tucson, Arizona 85721

Wendy Parent-Johnson, Ph.D., CRC, CESP, is executive director of the Sonoran UCEDD, a Center for Excellence in Developmental Disabilities, and professor, Department of Family & Community Medicine, College of Medicine, at the University of Arizona. Her educational background includes an M.S. degree in rehabilitation counseling and a Ph.D. in education with an emphasis on transition for individuals with severe disabilities, both from Virginia Commonwealth University. Dr. Parent-Johnson has 36 years' experience in the areas of supported and customized employment, transition from school to work, and Employment First policy and practice. Additionally, her research, teaching, and grant development has focused on health care transition, health disparities, interdisciplinary health science education, and the integration of health and employment. Dr. Parent-Johnson has conducted presentations and trainings; produced journal articles, book chapters, and other written products; and developed practical tools related to enhancing inclusive education, health care access, and employment outcomes. She is editor of the *Journal of Rehabilitation* and a member of the editorial board of the *Journal of Vocational Rehabilitation.*

Laura A. Owens, Ph.D., CESP
TransCen, Inc.
University of Wisconsin-Milwaukee
2400 E Hartford Ave
Milwaukee, Wisconsin 53211

Laura A. Owens, Ph.D., CESP, has over 30 years of experience as a national leader in the transition and disability employment field. She started her career as a teacher (both general and special education) and is currently a professor in the Department of Teaching and Learning at the University of Wisconsin–Milwaukee (UWM) where she coordinates the Graduate Transition Certificate program. She is the president of TransCen, Inc. (TCI), a national organization based in Rockville, Maryland, that provides direct placement services to individuals with disabilities; develops and evaluates new service models through research of evidenced-based practices leading to improved employment outcomes; and provides training and technical assistance to organizations and school districts focusing on the improvement of educational and employment outcomes for individuals with disabilities. In 1991, she founded Creative Employment Opportunities, Inc. (CEO) in Milwaukee, Wisconsin, an employment agency for individuals with disabilities, and ArtWorks for Milwaukee, a nonprofit jobs-training program in the arts for youth with and without disabilities in 2001. Dr. Owens served as the executive director of APSE, a national organization focusing on the advancement of integrated employment for citizens with disabilities based in Washington, DC, from 2008 to 2014, and along with Pat Keul and Wendy Parent-Johnson was instrumental in establishing the CESP, a national credential for employment support professionals. Dr. Owens is an internationally known speaker and has published widely on transition and employment topics. Laura earned her Ph.D. from the University of Wisconsin–Madison.

Richard Parent-Johnson, Ph.D.
University of Kansas
1450 Jayhawk Blvd
Lawrence, Kansas 66045

Richard Parent-Johnson, Ph.D., retired as a senior research associate in the Center for Disabilities in the Sanford School of Medicine, Vermillion, South Dakota. Prior to his position at Sanford, he was a senior research associate in the Center for Research on Learning at the University of Kansas and there held a courtesy appointment in the Department of Special Education. His doctorate is in sociology from the University of Kansas. Dr. Parent-Johnson has been the principal investigator (PI), co-PI, or project coordinator on multiple state and federal grants. His most recent work has focused on health care transitions for youth/young adults with disabilities as it relates to interprofessional medical education and clinical practice. He codesigned and then led the University of South Dakota's Center for Disabilities Transition *InAction* Clinic. He continues to do consulting work in these areas. Dr. Parent-Johnson's earlier work focused primarily on the iterative design, development, and dissemination of universal curricular products *and* processes that serve the individualized transition needs of persons with mild to moderate disabilities (e.g., the *Soaring to New Heights* curriculum and lesson materials for high-school-age students with disabilities and/or special health care needs). He also taught and served as the learning specialist at Seattle University. Dr. Parent-Johnson is knowledgeable in mixed methods research methodologies with particular expertise in ethnographic research and qualitative analysis.

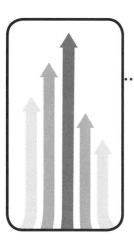

Preface

The goal of education is for all students to achieve their postsecondary education and/ or employment goals when they graduate. A proven predictor of postschool employment success for students with disabilities is having a job while in school–whether that is after-school work, weekend work, or summer jobs. It is important for school and adult service personnel to have high expectations, work together, share their resources, and utilize effective tools and practices to make postschool employment outcomes a reality.

One of the frustrations is when students graduate high school and have to start over in the adult system–encountering new assessments, new services, and new requirements that are often difficult to understand and navigate for everyone involved. Understanding what you as an educator or adult service professional can do to more effectively facilitate the process is one important element; understanding what the other does and authentically collaborating to ensure a successful transition to postschool employment is often the critical missing piece.

The framework for this book is based on lessons learned in our work in schools and adult services. Our focus intentionally blends both the educational and adult service worlds and provides proven materials that have been developed and utilized in schools and adult service agencies. Information and tools are presented with practical strategies for implementing in local communities and problem-solving issues that may be encountered. We hope that the resources and illustrations in this book will help students obtain better postschool employment options.

The authors of this book seek to describe, in ways that are meaningful for practitioners, strategies and tools to support youth in obtaining and maintaining employment. Each of the chapters collectively outline the transition process indicating the roles for school and adult services personnel in each of those areas. Working in unison to encourage high expectations and genuinely engage youth in their transition planning and services is at the heart of everything presented. Information is focused on providing pre-employment transition services (Pre-ETS), exploring interests and careers, connecting with the business community, accessing community-based work experiences, developing job opportunities, utilizing instructional and support strategies, and participating meaningfully with adult service agencies and other stakeholders. The Individualized Transition Action Plan (ITAP) developed together with the professionals responsible for transition services is introduced as a guide designed to help organize the process for professionals to plan, individualize, and implement the information and techniques presented throughout the book.

Our passion and experience in integrated employment spans over 30 years teaching, training, publishing, and actually providing employment services to young adults with disabilities across the country. We humbly offer our own lessons learned from those years here.

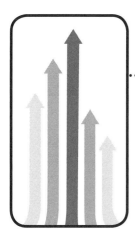

About the Downloads

Purchasers of this book may download, print, and/or photocopy the handouts and forms for educational use. These materials are included with the print book and are also available at www.brookespublishing.com/parent-johnson/materials for both print and e-book buyers.

Figure 2.3   Lesson Plan Form

Figure 2.4   Field Observation

Figure 3.2   Observation Template

Figure 3.3   Positive Personal Profile Form

Figure 3.4   Questions to Ask Supported Employment Providers

Figure 4.1   Job Observation Assessment Form

Figure 4.2   Consumer Situational Assessment Form

Figure 4.3   Situational Assessment Observational Form

Figure 4.4   Employee Progress Report

Figure 5.1   Networking

Figure 5.2   Informational Interview

Figure 5.4   Internship Business Partner Agreement

Figure 5.5   Worksite Analysis

Figure 5.6   Internship Performance Evaluation

Figure 5.7   Final Internship Evaluation

Figure 6.1   Task Analysis

Figure 6.2   Instructional Plan

Figure 6.3   Fading Plan

Figure 6.4   On-going Support Plan

Figure 7.1   Implementing Transition Action Plan (ITAP)

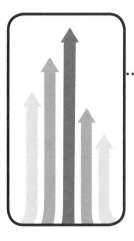

Acknowledgments

For decades we have met and worked with so many wonderful young adults with disabilities along with their teachers and employment consultants/job coaches. We would like to thank all of the individuals with disabilities we have worked with through the years who have taught us how to be better teachers and service providers. Through their determination in wanting a better life through employment, we have learned to push ourselves and others to ensure that employment for all really means all!

We would also like to thank Lee Bernfeld, a transition teacher in St. Francis, Wisconsin, and a UWM graduate student for his work ensuring our reference list was accurate!

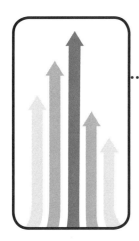

1

Getting Started

TRANSITION TO EMPLOYMENT

Educators play a significant role in changing the life trajectory of students with disabilities. No matter what their involvement is or the amount of time they have with a student, teachers can make a profound impact on their students' future employment. Teachers who have a student for only one year, one class period, or in an extracurricular activity they advise, may easily lose sight of the significance of their role. It is important to remember that transition to employment requires a coordinated set of future-driven and outcome-oriented activities. Outcomes (postschool outcomes guided by the dreams and goals of the student and his or her family) are often forgotten. The annual individualized education program (IEP) includes the objectives that form a blueprint to guide students during their school years to achieve their desired outcomes when they graduate. Each year must be purposeful in moving the students closer to their goals; each activity must be meaningful in relation to the bigger picture of a quality adult life. Teaching students direct skills, such as completing a particular task, and soft skills, such as interacting with others, is extremely important. Equally important are related skills such as acquiring a work ethic, identifying passions, enhancing self-efficacy, problem solving, dependability, and becoming a good coworker; these skills are often learned over time through the day-to-day experiences, role models, and real-life events encountered. All students can benefit from these opportunities, which should be a regular part of their education programming.

What if educators teach all these skills? What is the guarantee the student will become employed given the likelihood that other adult service professionals, who are not involved in the student's education, will be providing postschool employment-related services? These questions highlight another key point: collaboration. Transition, by definition, requires the involvement of many people in each student's life, including other school and adult service personnel. Working together with others enhances coordination, reduces gaps, and eliminates duplication. An added benefit to collaboration is the collective creativity, problem solving, resource development, and personnel support that a collaborative approach offers. Collaboration helps not only in the short term for an individual student but also in the long term for systemic change affecting all students. It simply is not effective for any school or adult service professionals to complete their roles in isolation of the others who are involved in transition. As the demand for integrated employment outcomes continues to grow and embrace more students, working together with others becomes a critical necessity. As an educator, it is important to be aware of the possible opportunities related to work, what services and supports are available, and what is needed to achieve employment. Regardless of who is responsible for implementing employment-related services, at a minimum, the educator's role is to coordinate the services, oversee their completion, and ensure that each service contributes to the larger picture.

Gaining knowledge and relationships around employment may feel like a big change if employment has not previously been a focus or a responsibility of teaching. Moving forward, consider these tips:

- Rather than planning for transition, focus on ACTION planning.

- Rather than assuming it will be done, focus on ensuring IMPLEMENTATION.

- Rather than checking off on process, focus on following up on OUTCOMES.

This book provides strategies for focusing on action, implementation, and outcomes. Information important for making employment a reality for students with disabilities is outlined in the practical strategies, tools, and examples presented throughout the book. While reading the book, it is important to distinguish between "need to know" and "need to do" based on your own situation and local community. Knowing what is required to transition to employment is the first step. Identifying what is being done and where gaps exist is an essential next step. Clarifying personal responsibilities is an important part of the process. Defining ways to address the gaps yourself or with others cannot be overlooked.

IMPORTANCE OF WORK

You may be asking, "Why work?" and "Why now?" After all, haven't educators always been charged with preparing our future citizens for college and the world of work? Since individuals with disabilities have been afforded a free and appropriate education with the passage of the Education of All Handicapped Children Act of 1975, great strides have been made in the outcomes experienced by students with disabilities. In higher numbers than ever before, students with disabilities are graduating from high school, going to college, and becoming employed. However, they are experiencing all of these outcomes at a rate much lower than their peers without disabilities (National Council on Disability, 2017; Newman et al., 2011; Wehman, 2013).

WHAT DO THE STATISTICS SAY?

Employment rates are still consistently lower for people with disabilities than for the population without disabilities. According to the Bureau of Labor Statistics (2019), the unemployment rate for individuals with a disability was 8.0% in 2018, more than twice that of those with no disability (3.7%). Individuals are counted as unemployed if they do not have a job, were available for work, and were actively looking for a job. It is important to note that there are many individuals with disabilities who are not employed and have given up looking for employment altogether. In 2018, 19.1% of individuals with disabilities were employed, whereas 65.9% of individuals without a disability were employed (Bureau of Labor Statistics, 2019). For individuals with intellectual and developmental disabilities (ID/DD), the number employed are even lower (Siperstein, Heyman, & Stokes, 2014). According to the 2016–2017 National Core Indicator data, a survey of 21,548 adults in 39 states served by ID/DD agencies reported 14.9% to be employed in individual paid jobs (National Association of State Directors of Developmental Disabilities Services & Human Services Research Institute, 2018; U.S.

Census Bureau, 2016). When looking at career development, individuals with a disability are often underemployed and tend to be working in service occupations (20.2%) compared to 17.3% of individuals without disabilities (Bureau of Labor Statistics, U.S. Department of Labor, 2019).

Individuals with a disability are less likely to work in management or professional occupations (34.1%) than are individuals without a disability (39.9%). The resulting impact of unemployment and underemployment is that individuals with disabilities experience poverty at a rate that is more than double that of the general population (Vallas & Fremstad, 2014). If you have a disability in the United States, you are twice as likely as a person without a disability to live in poverty, and that gap has widened in the 25 years since the landmark Americans with Disabilities Act was enacted (Fessler, 2015). Individuals with disabilities have generally poorer health, lower education achievements, fewer economic opportunities, and higher rates of poverty than do people without disabilities. Disability has a bidirectional link to poverty because it may increase the risk of poverty and poverty may increase the risk of disability (World Health Organization [WHO], 2011).

CHANGING THE LANDSCAPE OF DISABILITY AND EMPLOYMENT

Recent state and federal initiatives are focused on changing these outcomes. These initiatives have generated tremendous interest, increased expectations, and demonstrated successes emphasizing employment and the valued contributions made by workers with disabilities. A significant influence has been Employment First initiatives, which establish a framework for systems change centered on the presumption that all citizens, including individuals with significant disabilities, are capable of integrated employment (Association for Persons Supporting Employment First, n.d.). Employment First directives urge systems to align policies, service-delivery practices, and reimbursement structures to encourage integrated employment as the priority option for publicly funded services for youth and adults with significant disabilities (Office of Disability Employment Policy, n.d.). Today, all 50 states have some type of legislation, policy, or activity related to Employment First.

At the federal level, the passage of the Workforce Innovation & Opportunity Act (WIOA) (National Center on Leadership for the Employment and Economic Advancement of People with Disabilities, 2014) and the Centers for Medicare & Medicaid Services (CMS) final rule, which ensures that Medicaid's home- and community-based services programs provide full access to the benefits of community living and offers services in the most integrated settings, have changed the expectations and requirements of employment, particularly for transition-aged youth as they leave school. The question no longer is "Can this individual work?" but rather "How can we support this individual in work?"

The WIOA was signed into law by President Obama in 2014. The purpose of WIOA is to better align the workforce system with education and economic development in an effort to create a collective response to economic and labor market challenges on the national, state, and local levels (National Association of Workforce Boards, n.d.). Specifically, this legislation focuses on assisting job seekers with disabilities in succeeding in the labor market, matching employers with skilled workers who may benefit from education, skills training, and employment, and support services (National Center on Leadership for the Employment and Economic Advancement of People with Disabilities, 2014).

WIOA targets both in-school and out-of-school youth to assist them in their career and educational development. State vocational rehabilitation (VR) agencies must reserve funds for the sole purpose of providing Pre-Employment Transition Services (Pre-ETS). Whereas

VR has always provided transition services, WIOA expands the population of students to those who are eligible or who are potentially eligible for VR to receive services and permits a wider range of services to students with disabilities. Youth with disabilities do not need to be eligible for VR services as Pre-ETS can be provided to any student with a disability, regardless of whether the student has applied or been determined eligible for VR services. The five Pre-ETS services include

1. Job exploration counseling.

2. Work-based learning experiences, which may include in-school or afterschool opportunities, or experience outside the traditional school setting (including internships) that is provided in an integrated environment to the maximum extent possible.

3. Counseling on opportunities for enrollment in comprehensive transition or postsecondary educational programs at institutions of higher education.

4. Workplace readiness training to develop social skills and independent living.

5. Instruction in self-advocacy, which may include peer mentoring.

The requirement of Pre-ETS reinforces what research has demonstrated over the last several years regarding preparing students for competitive employment. Each of the five required Pre-ETS has been cited in research as a predicator of postschool success for students with disabilities. Additionally, the requirement of collaboration in implementing Pre-ETS focused on the outcome of employment has been cited in research as an effective practice (Fabian & Luecking, 2015; Test, Mazzotti, Mustain, Kortering, & Kohler, 2009).

This book reflects a different way of thinking, strategizing, and tackling the *very* diverse challenges faced in trying to help students make successful transitions from school to work. The essence of this difference can be expressed in two succinct sentences:

Bring the community into the classroom.

Take the classroom into the community.

Bringing the community into the classroom and taking the classroom into the community is about more than just making it real for students. It is about creating ways to evoke a personal response to the skills being taught and to the opportunities being provided. That is when learning will happen for all students!

Perhaps equally important is that when students are connected with the community of people and places important to their transition to employment (and further education), social capital is being developed. Social capital is the sum of the resources accumulated by an individual as he or she participates in a network of personal relationships of "mutual acquaintance and recognition" (Portes, 1998). For this population of students—most of whom have been marginalized in one way or another—building and accumulating social capital is critical for achieving access to and legitimacy in environments where they are relative newcomers (Parent-Johnson & Parent-Johnson, 2015).

Our premise is: Students who get connected to the broader community become engaged in the process of establishing and building social capital. By building this kind of social capital, they will gain the access, resources, and knowledge to function successfully in various environments with new expectations, roles, and rules that are different from those they have been accustomed to. As educators, our job is to facilitate this process and help students develop these connections into a durable network–a network that provides the means to achieve a successful and sustainable transition to employment (and more).

In addition, it is important to recognize that the professional and practical efforts required to bring the community into the classroom and the classroom into the community are different from the kind of participation that many educators have engaged in. The process requires the creation of an individual small community or team approach to address the issues at hand.

This process can–and in many situations should–start small. Putting together a team of two or three action-oriented colleagues who, together, identify a set of students and a set of goals they want to achieve is a first step. The number of active team members, the set of goals to achieve, and the number of students impacted can continue to grow on the basis of the team's experiences with what works and what more is needed.

This book contains a wide-ranging set of resources and practical ideas for getting the job done. But it is figuring out which resources and ideas to apply and how the team wants to orchestrate them into coherent actions that make the difference in the postschool outcomes for youth with disabilities. Precisely because this book includes so many ideas, it is important to be thoughtful about the specific goals the team sets for itself. Be purposeful and selective about setting goals relative to advancing the skills and opportunities provided for students to make strong and successful transitions.

Based on the team's expertise, determine the scope or list of topics to address, the necessary skills related to those topics, and the experiences that team members can provide relative to using those skills to connect students with the real-world community. Again, as a team, decide what topics, skills, and connecting experiences should come first and which ones should follow (building on the earlier experiences). Be creative; try new things and build on the efforts and activities that are working for the team. Most important, do not be afraid to revisit the team's original thinking and let the team-based process and content evolve.

UPCOMING CHAPTERS

Chapter 2 helps you think strategically about your plan to promote postschool employment. Chapter 3 continues the discussion of planning for employment by providing examples and tools, and it addresses interagency collaboration. Chapter 4 addresses the need to identify the passions of your students that lead to career exploration, and Chapter 5 focuses on developing employer relationships to provide employment opportunities based on student interests. Chapter 6 discusses how to provide support to students on the job to ensure skill development. Finally, Chapter 7 highlights some of the challenges and issues that may be experienced and provides effective strategies and solutions that other educators have suggested to help you move from "Can this individual work?" to "How can we support this individual in work?"

Chapter 7 also introduces the Implementing Transition Action Plan (ITAP)–offering readers a means to think through the transition process and concretely develop an action plan that provides guidance through the essential components of employment preparation and implementation, leading to truly integrated, competitive employment for students with disabilities.

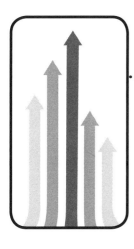

2

Strategies to Facilitate Effective Transitions

Stacy is one of a few high school special education instructors who has started integrating classroom and community experiences related to transition from school to employment for her junior class students. She describes these new activities as "formative education, not informative education." Stacy sees these experiences as initially being very foreign to young adults who are not used to participating at a personal level in class assignments. "This is often the first time many of my students have thought about most of these issues, let alone being asked to express themselves about them and begin to make 'choices' for themselves. It took them a while to realize that they 'could' learn how to do this stuff!" A particularly encouraging sign for Stacy was observing her students, after systematically analyzing and translating their IEPs into their own terms, begin to assert themselves in their IEP meetings and connect their learning goals with a job or future career beyond school.

The teacher in the vignette above is directly and purposefully engaged in helping her students gain the knowledge, experience, and sense of self-efficacy needed to make the successful transition from a school- and family-based environment to a more independent and self-determined world of education, employment, and life in general.

Making this transition is a profound change for everyone. For most students, it is a venture into the completely unknown territory of independence and adulthood. Increasingly, this time of transition is being recognized as a distinct life phase and is often described in terms of emerging adulthood (Arnett, 2000). As a life phase, this transition is understood and represented as an extended process—occurring between 14 and 26 years of age—rather than as a singular event at a given point in time.

For all students, this transition is a process that requires 1) a self-conscious exploration of themselves, 2) consistent guided practice at building the kinds of skills they will need to succeed, and 3) systematically structured opportunities for students to experience, test, and refine their own skills. For students with disabilities, creating and implementing this process is especially complicated—and necessary.

What follows in this chapter is a set of practical, field-tested strategies teachers can use to give their students the kind of knowledge, skills, and experiences they need to develop a positive and secure sense of their own capabilities to navigate this transition. But first, a point about the necessity of collaboration must be made.

THE CRUCIAL IMPORTANCE OF COLLABORATION

The transition we are talking about is a personal and practical journey through a diverse ecology of educational, organizational, health, and employment systems. Despite the Individuals with Disabilities Education Improvement Act 2004 (IDEIA) mandate that the "coordination of services with agencies involved in supporting the transition of students with disabilities to postsecondary activities" (20 U.S.C. 1411[d] § 300.704), these systems are *not* well integrated or coordinated.

It is clear that no one system, organization, or agency can be successful working on their own. One confirmation of this point comes from the National Collaborative on Workforce and Disability (NCWD):

> The diverse and often complex needs of youth who are transitioning to adulthood cannot be met by any one institution or service system alone. Most youth are served in some way by at least a few institutions and some youth are served simultaneously by many—schools, community-based programs, and service providers specific to health and mental health, social services, disability, child welfare, and juvenile delinquency prevention" (NCWD, 2016).

As suggested here, effective collaboration among all stakeholders would seem to be the obvious answer to such a dilemma. Indeed, NCWD/Youth labors diligently to increase collaboration in an effort to improve the quality and coordination of services, reduce duplication of effort, and narrow the gaps that obviously exist between services.

Unfortunately, the research on interagency collaboration and/or collaboration at the interprofessional level as they relate to transition is limited to a description of essential elements and functions of effective collaboration. Nevertheless, it is crucial that we recognize and continue to address the fact that teachers (and any other professionals engaged in this process with these emerging adults) need the time and the opportunity to work with other professionals.

Again, it is important to recognize that the challenges associated with these transitions are, themselves, multidimensional. Further, individuals in transition are also multidimensional in the sense that they embody a unique set of skills and experiences and therefore require genuinely individualized needs and supports. It is equally important to recognize that each separate organization engaged in supporting the overall transition process focuses on and serves a limited set of those needs. As a result of this silo effect, most of our government agencies and human services organizations are seemingly compelled to operate in cooperation with or in tandem with one another (Tett, 2015). The result is that our human services agency/educational/employment process has been constructed such that each part of the system does its own job and then hands off the client or student to the next organization or agency in line (Figure 2.1).

The hand-off model assumes a level of coherence and integration across organizations that simply does not exist. It can be argued that this hand-off model, whereby each part of the system deals with a subset of the issues that face the person, becomes a big part of the challenge faced by the person who is making the transition.

Cooperation between and among these entities is not enough. Facilitating these transitions must be more than a cooperative venture. To be successful, those transitions must become a genuine team-based collaborative process. It is important to recognize that the students themselves need to be at the center of the transition process. Perhaps even more important, we must recognize that these students need to learn how to participate at the center of that process and believe in their own capacity to do so.

Clearly, schools and human services agencies serve legitimately different roles and functions with regard to the transition process. As such, they have constructed many specialized

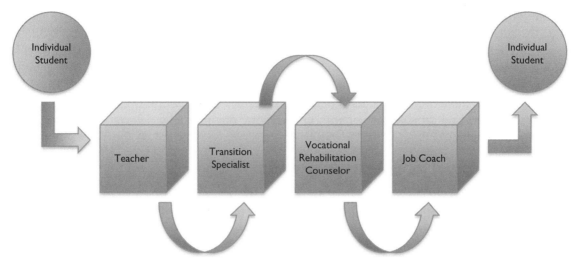

Figure 2.1. Hand-off model.

roles and functions within their systems; they have even constructed their own working vocabulary of terms and concepts that reflect and constrain their particular perspectives and goals. And yet, each agency or organization serves the same population of students! The real challenge, however, is that students, families, teachers, transition coordinators, adult services professionals, and vocational rehabilitation counselors alike must learn to navigate this fragmented environment.

It is not effective for each of these professionals to do their individual job in relative isolation from one another. It is not effective to create a transition process whereby students are handed off from one system or organization to another (and sometimes back and forth). What is needed is a genuinely collaborative approach that can respond to the multidimensional quality of the transition process (Antosh & Association of University Centers on Disabilities, 2013; Cobb & Alwell, 2009; Landmark, Ju, & Zhang, 2010; Noonan, Erikson, & Morningstar, 2012).

The literature is rife with various models of collaboration. Regardless of the particular version elaborated, each approach attempts to bring disparate systems, and the professionals working in each system, together in such a way that processes and services change for the better. One particularly interesting and successful model of collaboration has been developed by John Kania and Mark Kramer. In a series of articles in the *Stanford Social Innovation Review*, they define collaboration in terms of collective impact initiatives. That is, as "long-term commitments by a group of important actors from different sectors to a common agenda for solving a specific social problem. Their actions are supported by a shared measurement system, mutually reinforcing activities, ongoing communication, and are staffed by an independent backbone organization" (Kania & Kramer, 2011). Significantly, Kania and Kramer describe a set of essential elements that are critical to achieving and sustaining a coherent "alignment of effort" that leads to successful outcomes.

The definition and key practices of collective impact articulated by Kania and Kramer focus on large-scale change initiated at the macro (that is, systems and organizations) level. This is certainly an important and valuable perspective that will be addressed later in this chapter. However, the principles of collective impact also have powerful application at the micro level. That is, collective impact can be achieved in the field even when a small team of teachers, counselors, transition specialists, or other professionals work together to facilitate the successful transition of young adults with disabilities from education to employment or more education. What follows is a brief description of how to use the principles of collective impact to create and sustain a process that brings professionals together in a genuinely collaborative way that leads to more comprehensive and successful transitions for a common population of students and clients. This model of collaboration puts students/clients, as legitimate and capable participants, at the center of a mutually determined and responsive process (Figure 2.2).

GROW YOUR OWN COLLECTIVE IMPACT TEAM

Again, teachers, paraprofessionals, special education teachers, administrators, rehabilitation counselors, transition coordinators, and many other professionals are all engaged in some specific capacity in the effort to help students achieve good employment outcomes. However, the comprehensive nature of the challenges inherent in the goal of transitioning to employment works against the likelihood that any one individual can be successful by doing things on their own. The constraints on each professional's time and their own predetermined and defined roles relative to the student they are trying to serve—create a fragmented and poorly coordinated process that is often ineffective.

Any individual professional trying to make a positive impact on the trajectory of a student's life will find it is genuinely helpful, even necessary, to develop a more team-based approach. A single teacher can begin this process by seeking out and gaining the willing participation of one or two professionals in some other organization(s) outside the school system that have some professional stake in the successful transition outcome of these students (e.g., a rehabilitation counselor, transition specialist, or job coach). That new team needs to create a collective impact perspective as it relates to the challenges of transition at hand. In order to do that, the team members need to know how to collaborate or order to achieve a collective impact.

The research done by Kania and Kramer (2011) demonstrates that collective impact initiatives require the cumulative force of five specific conditions in order for them to be successful: 1) a common agenda, 2) shared measurement systems, 3) mutually reinforcing activities, 4) continuous communication, and 5) backbone support organization.

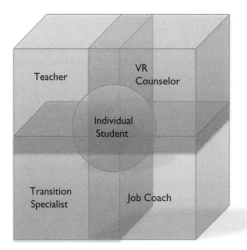

Figure 2.2. Collective impact team model.

COLLECTIVE IMPACT: A PRACTICAL APPLICATION

This section describes the five conditions and how they can be (and have been) applied in order to have a positive collective impact—in this case, on the goal of achieving the successful transition from school to employment for students with disabilities. This description is intended as a guide for how to initiate and sustain the conditions necessary to achieve a collective impact. As a guide, it is not intended to be complete and comprehensive. Rather, the content and activities suggested here are concrete, practical ways a small group of professionals can create an impact on the outcomes as students transition from school to employment that is greater than the sum of their individual efforts. View these materials as a resource and base from which to orchestrate your own collective impacts.

First, it is important to understand that creating a truly collaborative agenda and participating in mutually reinforcing activities are actually parts of a single, dynamic process. That is, a common agenda is the result of participating in mutually reinforcing activities. To begin the process, seek out and gain the willing participation of one or two other professionals from outside your own field. For example, a high school special education teacher might consider inviting a vocational rehabilitation counselor, a job coach, and/or an employment specialist to become team participants. Team members need to determine among themselves what their overall goals will be. Create a set of goals all members share. For example, which students do you want to focus on? Do you want to improve the overall self-determination skills of each student? Or, are there particular skills that you deem to be most important for students to improve or perfect? Discuss the types of skills and activities you want your students to accomplish. This represents the scope or range of the skills and activities you and your team want to achieve together with your students.

Curriculum developers often talk about the scope and sequence aspects of course content. This conversation is critical for the collective impact team to have. Developing the scope of the course content simply means determining what lessons and skills should be taught and when. Developing the sequence of activities of those lessons means determining when and in what order those lessons and skills should be taught. Drafting and working to perfect the scope and sequence of lessons and experiences in providing transition services is something that must be done by all the collective impact team members together. Developing an effective collective impact team requires both time and practice. Recognize that this is going to require at least a modest time commitment from all team members. Questions to address include: What are the key lessons and skills students need? How many and what kind of experiential learning events does the team believe will advance the students' functional skills and understanding of the worlds of work and/or education they have ahead of them? What other skills and experiences does the team deem critical to this goal? What lessons and experiences within and beyond the classroom will support that learning?

Make some initial decisions about these issues. Then begin your move toward a common agenda. A common agenda is more than a set of abstract goals that is mutually agreed upon at the initial stages of working together. It is not something that is achieved in the abstract. A common agenda is a shared vision that emerges and continues to evolve over time. It comes about as a result of spending time together—participating in an intentional and purposeful way in one another's professional roles and activities. It is the outcome of the work you do in terms of mutually reinforcing activities. Thus, the scope and sequence of your cumulative program will be subject to change as the team learns what is most effective for them.

A *comprehensive* set of lessons or topics that addresses the multiple skills and activities students would benefit from relative to making effective transitions is included here. The lessons and topics are arranged as four units with a specific content and sequence that represents best practice as it has emerged in other transition-focused educational settings. The units were developed and implemented as a semester-long curriculum for a class of 10 to 12 high-school-age students. They are recommended as a starting point from which your own team can decide what lessons and topics you want to address with your own students. Each unit has a specific theme and its own unique *guiding question* that should be introduced to the students and repeated on a routine basis. Within any given unit the number of topics and activities you address will depend upon the time you have with your students and how much time you devote to any individual topic.

Unit 1: Discovering My Own Path

Guiding Question: What does it mean to transition, and how can I understand myself in those terms?

Suggested topics and activities:

- Define the concept and common experience of transitions.

- Describe the particular transition from school to work and what it involves.

- Introduce the members of the transition team.

- Discuss general substance of IEP with each student individually.

- Use specific tools/lessons to help students identify their strengths.

- Use specific tools/lessons to help students identify and explore their interests.

- Discuss and help students understand the financial benefits of work.

- Enhance each student's disability awareness, e.g., Americans with Disabilities Act (ADA), IDEIA, and their rights.

- Explore and enhance individual effective communication skills (e.g., FACTS; see Figure 2.5).

Unit 2: Charting My Own Course

Guiding Question: Where do I want to go in life and what steps can I take that will help get me there?

Suggested topics and activities:

- Discuss life values and how they can work to guide our direction in life.

- Discuss and help students create their own individual mission statements.

- Discuss the critical importance of setting goals.

- Use specific goal-setting lessons to help students learn how to set goals.

- Discuss the importance of the *student's own role* in pursuing their goals.

- Discuss and teach students the use of short-term and long-term goals.

- Use specific tools/lessons to teach and practice time management skills, including learning how to prioritize their time into a day and a week.

Unit 3: Taking Real Action

Guiding Question: How can I best share information about myself and build my own team that helps support me in reaching my goals?

Suggested topics and activities:

- Discuss and teach how to become a self-advocate!

- Teach and facilitate each student to write a basic resume.

- Teach students how to interview in ways that communicate your strengths.

- PRACTICE interviewing.

- Teach students how to handle tough personal questions.

- Demonstrate and practice filling out job applications.

- Demonstrate and practice the art of networking.

- Anticipate and plan for transportation issues.

Unit 4: Getting to My Destination

Guiding Question: How can I get <u>and</u> keep the job I want and stay on track for reaching my goals?

Suggested topics and activities:

- Discuss what a dream job might look like.

- Teach and practice networking with people who do the work you want to do.

- Job shadow people who do the kind of work you want to do

- Discuss what community resources and agencies exist to support students.

- Bring two or three employers in to share what they value in their employees.

- Celebrate each student's success!

As part of the scope and sequence process, it is important for the collective impact team to develop a calendar of these kinds of activities, especially those that are going to include students. It is an invaluable planning tool that keeps all team members organized and on the same page relative to what each member needs to do to make things happen. The calendar is useful not only for planning purposes but also to help students see the logic behind these kinds of explorations. It is important for students to see that they are building toward a coherent package of experiences and skills that will benefit them in the long run.

One additional tool that will become a valuable asset to both teachers and students alike is to create a lesson plan for most topics that are chosen to be addressed. It takes a bit of work on the part of at least one team member, but creating a lesson plan provides a clear focus and objective to each lesson. For example, see the lesson plan document shown in Figure 2.3.

Perhaps the most effective strategy to achieve a truly common agenda and set of practices that focus on individual goals is to create opportunities for students to act as participant-observers of the official roles that each of the team members perform. For example, teachers can create opportunities to bring vocational rehabilitation counselors into the classroom as participant-observers when information is communicated and the skills appropriate for

Lesson Plan Form

Guiding Question
Example: What does it mean to be "SELF-determined," and how can I begin to understand myself in those terms?

_____

_____

Focus Question
Example: What students and staff should I expect to work with during this course, and what are their roles in my education?

_____

_____

Objective
Example: Students and staff share general information about themselves in an effort to become aware of the people involved in the class.

_____

_____

Description
Example: This lesson is designed to help students learn about themselves, each other, and the staff. They will become acquainted with the other people who will be in the classroom on a daily basis. Students have the opportunity to identify commonalities with other students. Formal and informal assessment material will also be completed by the student and/or guardian to assess levels of self-efficacy and determination.

_____

_____

Classroom Activities

_____

_____

_____

Review and Reflect
- What did you learn?
- Where do we go from here?

Wrap Up and Teacher Notes

_____

_____

_____

Looking Ahead
Date of agency staff visit (Vocational rehabilitation, workforce center, life skills staff): _____

_____

Date and name of guest speakers: _____

Date and location of off-campus site visits: _____

Figure 2.3. Lesson plan form.

transitioning to the workplace or some form of postsecondary education are taught. At a separate class session, introduce the counselors and ask them to describe their roles and what they can do for students. As a team, participate in activities with the students that involve all or combinations of team members.

Conversely, create opportunities for teachers to become participant-observers of the vocational rehabilitation counselors as they function on the job. For example, teachers can visit a counselor's office to better understand their colleague's role, practices, and work environment. The point is that it is important to know each other's worlds. An interesting and valuable follow-along activity to this initial action can then be a student and/or class experience whereby the counselor hosts a student or the class in a hands-on experience of the office. There, students can have a face-to-face encounter with the people and practices that are there to serve their interests.

A teacher can bring a counselor or adult services professional into the classroom to talk about employment options, to inform students about or perhaps initiate student enrollment in services. Over time, the counselor or adult services professional and the students become more familiar with one another; each learns more personal aspects about the other. In this way, the all-important element of trust between counselor and students is developed. Collaboratively, the teacher and counselor can begin thinking about how they might match individual students to different job opportunities, how certain skills might be taught to the class of students, and how specific skills could be nurtured in specific students. Together, they might even coordinate at least a few students with real job exploration opportunities that allow all parties to see what makes a good fit for that student and what the student might need for support in order to succeed in that opportunity.

Each student who participates in this activity or in any other off-campus activity should be required to complete some kind of assessment or evaluation of their experiences in the field. Completing a simple, concrete document (Figure 2.4) helps them think about and articulate a meaningful, personal connection between what they saw or heard and what they think about it. It also provides them a record of their experience and thoughts that they can use to compare jobs in terms of pros and cons and that can be included in a transition portfolio.

The experiences that students encounter as part of those job exploration opportunities should definitely become part of structured discussions in later classes. That is, as a group, students should be asked to share their experience and to consciously explore their experience and what meaning it has for them now and in the future. This same kind of purposeful site-visit activity can also be applied to visits to local community colleges and businesses.

Over time, given the opportunity to be participant-observers in one another's worlds, not only does each professional learn more about each other's roles and practices, but there is also a kind of hybridization of roles. What emerges from these opportunities is a new shared experience and a common shared language to articulate and facilitate transition practices for both groups of professionals. Transition practices become team based and comanaged rather than a set of institutionalized hand-offs.

One of the important changes to emerge from observing other systems, particularly for special education teachers, rehabilitation counselors, and transition specialists is the change in mindset these professionals often have as a result of working in a more personal and holistic way with students. In the everyday work world, it is not uncommon for professionals to have high student–staff ratios, extensive caseloads, and heavy workloads in general. As hardworking professionals, they are compelled to focus their efforts on discrete aspects of a student's life. While this is a professional and practical necessity, what can and does get lost

Field Observation

❏ Business   ❏ Educational   ❏ Training Site   ❏ Housing Community

Place: _____ Date: _____

	Like	OK	Do Not Like	Comments
The **Place**				
The **People:** Supervisors/administrators Coworkers/classmates (Use comments section to add contact information)				
The **Programs:** Work/educational				They are:
Overall Impression				Because:

Questions I have about this job, training, or program:

_____

_____

_____

Possible questions to ask:
- It would be nice if this place had _____. Does it? Why or why not?
- What are the costs?
- How long will the training take?
- When could I move in?

1. _____

2. _____

3. _____

4. _____

5. _____

Figure 2.4. Field observation form.

is the sense of that student as a whole person. When these same professionals are allowed the opportunity to teach a course that addresses the whole person—in classes of 10 students that meet three times per week for a semester—the teachers and the counselors are, themselves, changed. The experiences they have working with students in this more whole-person way coalesces into a time of powerful and gratifying professional growth.

INTEGRATING BEST PRACTICES

There are a myriad of best practices that teachers, paraprofessionals, special education teachers and administrators, transition coordinators, rehabilitation counselors, and many other professionals can and should adopt in order to help students achieve good employment outcomes. This section offers a set of key teaching and learning principles specific to teaching students with disabilities and provides examples of how these strategies have been operationalized and integrated into everyday practice. The key principles are 1) focusing on self-efficacy, including modeling, role playing, and elaborated feedback; 2) knowing how you and your students learn; 3) learning as a social and guided activity; and 4) using Universal Design for Learning (UDL).

For over 20 years, there has been a concerted effort in special education to improve the self-determination skills of students with disabilities (Mithaug, 1993, 1996; Mithaug, Agran, Martin, & Wehmeyer, 2003; Wehmeyer, 1996, 1997, 1999, 2006; Wehmeyer, Yeager, Bolding, Agran, & Hughes, 2003). A strong case has been made that improving the attitudes and abilities, including self-advocacy, choice making, problem solving, self-awareness, and self-efficacy, of students with disabilities will improve overall life outcomes for students. As a result, scores of classroom curricula and larger programmatic efforts have focused on the development of self-determination skills. Identifying and improving upon self-determination skills is now common practice. It has been and still is recognized as best practice. However, what is often routinely assumed, and therefore overlooked in the content and practice related to self-determination, is attention to the sense of self-efficacy many of these students have. It is argued here that rather than being one of the elements subsumed within the model of self-determination, self-efficacy must be understood as a prerequisite to learning and achieving a self-determined life.

Self-efficacy is the sense of being capable of actually doing what is expected. Bandura defines self-efficacy as "one's perceived capabilities for learning or performing tasks at designated levels" (Bandura, 1997, p. 3). However, many students with disabilities do not have a strong sense of self-efficacy; that is, they do not see themselves as capable learners. It is very unlikely that adolescent students will persist in trying to learn any activity when feeling incompetent is their experience and their expectation. Given this essential perception of self, it is critical that addressing and then building a sense of self-efficacy in students needs to happen before teaching self-determination skills (Pajares & Urdan, 2006).

It is important to recognize that self-efficacy is not a generalized sense of confidence or self-esteem. Self-efficacy is a person's perception of himself or herself as being capable of learning or doing a particular task. The important focus, then, is on finding ways to support and enhance students' experience of being capable of doing the tasks that are asked of them. When it comes to learning and work environments, three teaching strategies—when used routinely and over time—are especially effective: 1) modeling, 2) role playing, and 3) elaborated feedback. Students with disabilities, in particular, need to 1) see or hear models of thinking and doing a task, 2) get real-time practice at doing the task, and 3) receive high-quality feedback on their performance.

Modeling

To model a skill or activity in the sense used here means to demonstrate the skill or activity while you literally *think aloud*. In practical terms, this means 1) describing the skill or activity in some basic detail, 2) stating why the skill is useful, 3) explaining when the skill is useful, and 4) performing the skill yourself from start to finish while sharing your own thinking out loud. The purpose is to demonstrate, out loud, your own thinking, your own problem solving, and even your own stops and starts as you perform the task. This demonstration is an out-loud model of the particular skill your students are expected to learn—against which they can compare and gauge their own performance.

For example, an invaluable strategic learning lesson was developed by faculty at the Center for Research on Learning at the University of Kansas (Lancaster & Johnson, 2005) on how to perform effectively during a job interview. The lesson involves teaching students five key steps to achieving a good interview and how to perform them. The five elements are 1) **F**ace the person, 2) **A**ctivate eye contact, 3) **C**heck expressions, 4) **T**alk clearly, and 5) **S**tay calm. There is a value-added aspect to this particular lesson in that it has its own acronym. That is, each piece of the lesson on good interviewing skills has its own phrase to describe it. The first letter from each phrase forms the acronym FACTS that helps students to more easily recall the entire set of actions they should do in order to perform effectively in any interview.

Modeling this lesson, the teacher chooses a student to sit across from him or her and plays the role of interviewee by having the student read a few predetermined questions commonly asked in an interview. In response to the questions, the teacher performs each step of the FACTS strategy—sometimes in a positive way (e.g., facing the person and making eye contact) and sometimes in a poor way (e.g., mumbling, looking out the window, and/or acting very anxious). All the while, the teacher can sustain a running commentary on which step is being modeled and why he or she is acting in a particular way.

Interestingly, the FACTS routine started out as a strategy for learning effective interviewing skills. However, in many classes it has become the standard of practice for any lesson in which students are asked to communicate directly with one another (i.e., it can become a class norm). For example, teachers may create a poster-size illustration of the FACTS routine and hang it on the classroom wall for use all year round (Figure 2.5).

Remember, as a part of any modeling activity, the *think aloud* strategy is an invaluable element for facilitating effective learning in nearly all settings. It has an infinite number of applications and should be considered a standard practice for teaching and learning.

Role Playing by Students

Many people learn best when given the opportunity to try things out in a hands-on way. For that reason, the value of practicing/performing an activity or abstract lesson is hard to overestimate. It is one thing to hear a lecture on a subject or to read directions on how to do something; it is quite another to actually try to do it. For most people, hearing, reading, and doing is an ideal combination of activities that serves to optimize the effectiveness of learning. Consider the FACTS interviewing skills lesson. The FACTS lesson should first be described to students in terms of its five elements; followed by a brief discussion of why, when, and where this skill is useful; and then modeled for the students. The culminating action, however, is to have students role-play this lesson. In particular, students should take turns playing three different roles: interviewee, interviewer, and observer. Being the interviewee gives a student practice at responding to the kinds of real questions they are most likely to face in an

1) **FACE** the person

2) **ACTIVATE** eye contact

3) **CHECK** expression

4) **TALK** clearly

5) **STAY** calm

Figure 2.5. FACTS poster.

interview process and helps them learn to frame and express their responses in more precise ways. Then, by doing a role reversal and playing the role of the interviewer, these same students can gain valuable new insights. Being the interviewer puts students on the other side of the conversation; they often discover something about what it looks and feels like to have someone respond to their questions and what can come through as effective or ineffective communication. Finally, taking a turn at being an impartial observer while two other people perform the interview provides the opportunity for the student to see the whole dynamic of give and take between the interviewer and interviewee. They can then offer their comments in an effort to give helpful feedback to the interviewees.

While this can be a fun activity, one additional point is necessary to make. With practice over time, students will become increasingly articulate and comfortable in their performances. It is important to recognize the necessity of providing the right environment for performing role plays. Regardless of their role, every performer needs to feel safe. All performers need to be respectful of one another and the roles they are performing. Only then will their comfort and skill grow.

Elaborated Feedback

All students need feedback on their performance. Feedback is especially important to students with a diminished sense of self-efficacy. For that reason, providing high-quality feedback is a key strategy for supporting not just students' comprehension of a particular lesson but also their perception of themselves as a capable learner.

We are all familiar with the concept of feedback. Providing feedback, both formally and informally, has become a common practice in everyday life, both personal and professional. Retailers and service providers often ask us to provide feedback in the form of telephone or online surveys. Colleagues and supervisors solicit feedback from us as well. Certainly, providing feedback has long been an integral part of any teaching and learning environment. However, not all feedback is of equal value and quality. In an effort to understand and refine the structure and practice of good-quality feedback, the Center for Research on Learning at the University of Kansas researched and developed a process called *elaborated feedback* (Kline, Schumaker, & Deshler, 1991) as part of a set of tools that demonstrate effectiveness with learners with special needs.

Elaborated feedback has a few key elements, each one of which is important to consider. In essence, elaborated feedback means 1) providing a one-on-one meeting with the student, 2) offering at least three positive statements about the student's performance, 3) identifying not the number of errors but the *type* of error the student made, 4) giving examples of the correct performance regarding the error type, 5) describing how to avoid the error in the future, and 6) having the student say back what he or she just heard.

Learn How You and Your Students Learn

The ways and means by which people learn are highly individualized. There are valid and meaningful ways to understand learning style, and it is much more than an abstract label. It can be understood quite literally as the way individuals perceive information, how they process the information, and what they do with that information. People develop their learning style over time and become comfortable using it. It represents their default method of learning. That is, because an individual's learning style represents his or her comfort zone, it is where he or she prefers to begin the activity of learning something new.

While the concept of learning styles is not scientifically validated, it is certainly a useful and fun way for students and teachers to engage in valuable conversations about how each of us approach learning new things—regardless of the context. There are a number of instruments that can be used to understand how a person learns. One instrument especially useful in secondary and postsecondary educational settings is the Kolb Learning Style Inventory (Kolb & Kolb, 2005). It asks individuals to rank their preferences to a set of questions that address learning situations. From their composite scores, the scale identifies students as one of four styles of learners, X, Y, Z, or A. Each learning style is articulated as having a particular set of strengths and limitations that tend to surface or get expressed in different learning situations. No one style fits, or is effective, in all situations.

Another online instrument out of the University of North Carolina, the *Index of Learning Styles* (Felder & Silverman, 2002), provides an indication of a student's learning preferences by identifying preferences on four dimensions: 1) active/reflective, 2) sensing/intuitive, 3) visual/verbal, and 4) sequential/global. A student's learning style profile provides the student (and you) with a list of possible strengths as well as tendencies that might lead to difficulty in academic settings. A note of caution: Findings should not be used to determine a student's suitability or unsuitability for a particular subject or career goal. As with any learning style tool, the results should not be overinterpreted but should be used as a guide. If a student does not agree with the findings, trust his or her judgment over the instrument results.

Clearly, knowing how individual students learn is invaluable to any teacher. However, one of the most easily overlooked parts in the learning–teaching equation is how you, the teacher, learn. How you teach is going to be strongly influenced by your own learning style. For example, your starting point and the strategies you use in your opening approach to a new concept or subject often come from your own learning comfort zone. Your learning style reflects how you perceive and process the information you are presenting. In other words, you tend to teach the way you learn best. This is why it is critical for you to know your own learning style. Reflect on how your style influences not only the methods you use to teach a lesson but also what you value in terms of how the students demonstrate their competency in a subject.

The overall message to students is that it is good to know and use their own learning style but also to be capable of developing and adapting to other styles of learning as well. The message for the teacher is to create learning environments where all learning styles are valued and each learner is given the opportunity to at least begin any learning activity in a way that fits his or her individual learning style.

Regardless of the means by which each student's learning style is determined, a very useful strategy is to create learning teams where each team comprises students who represent different learning styles. Provide each team a particular problem to solve or address. Within teams, each student is expected to bring the strength of his or her learning style to the problem-solving process and to consciously observe the strengths of other team members during the activity/discussion. Learning through consciously observing and participating with one another in this team approach validates students' individual learning styles and exposes them to the strengths of other approaches to learning.

Learning as a Social and Guided Activity

It is important to remember that we are social beings and that learning as a part of our social interactions with others is a continuous experience. The real challenge faced by a teacher is how to organize team-based activities in such a way that students have a structure and process they will actually use. Students can, indeed, be taught how to function effectively together as part of a small group or team. They can learn that by working together, they often accomplish more and better things than they would have been able to do alone. To be successful, a team-based learning process must be simple and straightforward. And it must be practiced until it becomes a matter of routine.

Palincsar, Magnusson, Cutter, and Vincent (2002) developed a team-based strategy that relies on a guided-inquiry model of teaching and learning. Operationalizing its most basic steps, the guided-inquiry model contains six key elements: 1) The teacher introduces a subject or topic for the day and asks a question that focuses on some key aspect of the subject; working within small groups, students 2) frame the question in their own words; 3) look for evidence that, in their minds at least, deals with the question at hand; 4) use their evidence to develop an answer to the question; 5) report to the whole class what their particular group has determined to be the answer to the question—including the evidence they used to support their answer; and 6) respond respectfully to the first group's conclusions, agreeing or disagreeing with them and indicating why.

One attempt to integrate several of the themes discussed here is represented in Box 2.1. This outline blends the key elements of modeling with the process of guided inquiry whereby the teacher becomes the facilitator of a community of practice that, with time and patient practice, is progressively more student driven.

Box 2.1   A Teaching Model for Student-Driven Learning and Community

Teacher Driven

  I. Describe

  II. Model

  III. Practice

  IV. Guided-inquiry process—in response to a focus question, the teacher facilitates small groups of students to

     A. Take a position/complete a task

     B. Specify what supports the group's position/task

     C. Defend the group's position (aloud to others)

  V. Over time, this learning dynamic generates a community of practice that is student driven; the teacher acts as facilitator

  VI. Individual products and actions

Develop and/or Use Universally Designed Methods and Materials

The racial, cultural, language, and ability diversity found in classrooms and other learning environments today is greater than ever before, and that diversity is increasing exponentially. To be successful in everyday reality, teachers must match that diversity with their own diversity of methods and materials they use to engage and teach students. Remember, there is no single way to learn and demonstrate competency of understanding and performance.

It is now imperative that a universal design approach be applied to curricula, teaching, and classrooms. That means processes and products need to be designed and delivered "that are usable by people with the widest possible range of functional capabilities" (Assistive Technology Act of 1998, 29 U.S.C. 3002[a][17]).

This mandate has been embodied in three key principles that are the core elements of UDL: 1) multiple means of representation to give learners various ways of acquiring information and knowledge; 2) multiple means of expression to provide learners alternatives for demonstrating what they know; and 3) multiple means of engagement to tap into learners' interests, challenge them appropriately, and motivate them to learn.

When developing classroom materials and methods, it is critical to understand that diverse materials need to be developed—all of which address the same lesson and have the same goals for learning. Some students may access the lesson content and demonstrate competency in having learned it with one type or combination of materials better than another. For example, visual/graphic representation of concepts is often more accessible than verbal/textual content to students with disabilities.

One critical but often overlooked and/or underutilized strategy for universalizing a classroom and lesson content is the development of a glossary of key terms that is specifically related to the lesson being taught. The glossary should identify critical terms, define them in everyday English and any other language needed, and include some graphic representation or illustration of the term if possible (Figure 2.5 presented earlier in the chapter is an example of this). One point of emphasis is important here. Words or concepts seldom have a simple, direct translation from one language to another. It is a mistake to assume there is common understanding for particular concepts or terms that can be applied for all students. Cultural and/or intellectual differences prevail. An effective glossary of key terms should be developed that includes symbols and/or synonyms for each word or concept listed. When necessary, it should also be multilingual. Finally, each glossary needs to be developed and made publicly available (e.g., make it a poster) to all students. In fact, working with students to create this glossary can be a valuable class activity itself.

Collective Impact at the Organizational Level

Public-private, multistakeholder efforts to cooperate with one another in an earnest effort to solve a problem or at least address a significant issue have existed for decades. Yet, as Kania and Kramer (2011) indicate, the history of the vast majority of these initiatives suggests they have met with limited success. In general, these partnering cooperative initiatives routinely exhibit many of the following shortcomings:

• They are often targeted too narrowly and do not engage a sufficiently comprehensive set of the affected stakeholders.

• While participants may organize around a particular theme or goal, they wrongly assume that all participants have a common understanding of what that theme or goal actually means.

• The cooperation/collaboration is ad hoc, and emphasis is most often focused simply on information sharing and particular short-term actions.

• Communication among participants is limited in scope and frequency.

• Participants do not adopt an evidence-based plan of action and/or develop a shared means for measuring outcomes/impact.

• There is limited infrastructure to support the work and/or initiate accountability for results.

The same five elements needed to create a successful collective impact that were introduced earlier in this chapter can be applied here—only this time at the macro level. Again, the necessary conditions include having 1) a common agenda, 2) mutually reinforcing activities, 3) continuous communication, 4) shared measurement systems, and 5) backbone support organization(s).

This section describes how the five conditions can be addressed at the macro level—that is, at the large, organizational level relative to the work these organizations have in relation to a common set of students whom they are serving. It is a description of the kinds of activities that can lead to the development of a positive collective impact on the goal of supporting the effective transition of students from school to employment—at the organizational level. As in the earlier sections, this description is intended to act as a guide for how to initiate and sustain the conditions necessary to achieve a collective impact. As a guide, it is not intended to be complete and comprehensive. Rather, these activities suggest important ways a group of organizations can move beyond cooperation to actually creating a collective impact on the transition of students from school to employment that is greater than the sum of the efforts made by their individual organizations.

Again, it is important to understand that creating a truly collaborative agenda that has a collective impact comes about when groups create a common agenda that is the result of participating in mutually reinforcing activities. It is far more than basic cooperation.

Earlier, it was described how a single professional can begin this process by seeking out and gaining the willing participation of another professional in some other organization outside the school system who has some stake in the successful transition outcome of these students (e.g., a rehabilitation counselor). Moving beyond that, organizations can collectively develop a more systemic response to the same goals. How this might happen is discussed next.

Create a Truly Common Agenda

Perhaps the single most significant action to take to address the challenge of navigating this terrain of separate, diverse, and specialized organizations is to create opportunities for key professionals (i.e., teachers, transition coordinators, vocational counselors, and others) who are engaged in the transition process to 1) develop a more complete understanding of one another and the separate institutions they work in and 2) create a common vision for these students that includes a shared set of steps/actions and a shared vocabulary of terms to articulate the vision.

This means bringing together a group that includes key decision makers, that is, people holding positions of authority, from the various organizations and agencies relevant to supporting successful transitions. This group must also include representatives of those agencies who are actually putting the team vision into practice—the teachers, transition specialists, vocational counselors, and so on. It will be the responsibility of this second set of representatives to report back the activities and results of everyday work in the field to the whole team. That is, they provide a kind of feedback loop with regard to successes and failures or shortcomings of everyday practices related to the model of what the larger group has developed. Changes to the model, if deemed necessary by the larger group, will be developed on the basis of feedback coming to them from the field.

All organizations have a standard of practice, a set of rules and regulations within which they operate, and a time line for achieving the actions related to the goals of their organization. They also have their own vocabulary to communicate their rules and activities. It is critical for all organizations working together not only to articulate their own rules and vocabularies to one another but also to make certain that there is a shared understanding of them. Once all participating organizations have articulated their relevant individual goals, rules, and regulations to the other groups, they have to come to an out-loud articulation of what they have as a goal for their work. For example, it is one thing for a group of organizations to recognize that they are all part of a generalized process of helping students successfully transition from school to work—but what transition actually means to each organization can be quite different. Those differences need to be discussed until a truly shared meaning of transition has been articulated to the satisfaction of all members of the group. This seemingly small act is critical because it ultimately determines how a successful transition will be recognized and measured.

Establish a Shared Measurement System

It is vital for this team to define, in advance of work in the field, how they want to measure the success of their efforts. Is success to be measured in terms of employment outcomes? What defines employment, and when is that outcome to be measured? Or, is success to be measured in terms of skill development—say, for example, in terms of students becoming more self-determined? If so, can a pre- and postmeasure of self-determination be administered? Which one? When? By whom? These are important questions that need to be identified and answered. The participation—not only of the students, teachers, and counselors, but of the organizations themselves—may be predicated on the outcomes to those measures.

Participate in Mutually Reinforcing Activities

Participate as a whole collective impact team in the marketing of its vision and activities. This means that high-level organization members find and/or create opportunities to meet the public—students, parents, and other organizations—to share the vision, the goals, and the practices of their efforts. It is this listening to and participating with one another that reinforces the common message and outcomes they have come together to create and support.

Maintain Continuous Communication

Finally, it is suggested that for collective impact activities to be most effective, regular meetings with representatives from all levels of participation should occur. For example, a broad-reaching transition project in Wichita, Kansas, brought together the state Kansas Rehabilitation Services, the Kansas Health Policy Authority, and the Wichita Public School District #259. Meetings that included director-level administrators from all three organizations—as well as representatives of the teachers and rehabilitation counselors working in the field/classroom—were held monthly. This was seen as the best way to ensure a consistent and reliable method of keeping all participants, regardless of their role, in step with one another. In general, team members must communicate routinely and in such a way that they inform one another about what is actually going on in the field and in each organization. Clearly, sometimes what is needed in the field requires decisions and actions at the organizational level in order to improve practices and outcomes. Similarly, if the organizations have rules and regulations that dictate activities in a formal way, those requirements will inform practices in the field. Regardless of which level is the focus or the determinant of the practices in the field, the point remains that these are all attempts at collective actions. A minimum requirement for the collective impact team as a whole should be monthly meetings. Some members of the team should anticipate meeting more frequently than that.

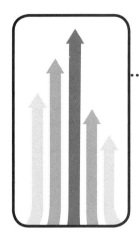

3

Planning for Employment: Person-Centered Planning and Adult Agency Involvement

Ms. Anderson was working with Dudley, a student with a mild intellectual disability and cerebral palsy, who used an electric wheelchair for mobility. Dudley was moving into his last year of school, so Ms. Anderson reached out to a local adult service organization that provided integrated employment services for individuals with disabilities. Ms. Anderson, Dudley, and Larry, from the adult services organization met and discussed conducting a person-centered planning (PCP) meeting with Dudley to guide in the development of an individualized transition action plan. The first step was for Ms. Anderson to work with Dudley and identify the people in his life he wanted to invite to his PCP meeting. A date and location were agreed upon, and Dudley, with support from Ms. Anderson, developed invitations that he delivered in person and e-mailed to possible attendees. The invitations included a brief description of the purpose of the meeting; the date, time, and location of the meeting; and an RSVP so Dudley could keep track of who would attend. The meeting occurred on a Saturday morning at a local library in the community in which Dudley lived. Dudley's family (parents and siblings), friends, teachers, and a neighbor attended the meeting. Larry facilitated the meeting discussion, and Dudley assisted. Larry began the meeting by asking Dudley to introduce everyone and explain why they were important in his life. Larry then facilitated using poster paper to document all the information from the discussions (see Box 3.1). After the meeting, Larry wrote a summary, including the action plan, and met with Ms. Anderson and Dudley to review. It was clear from the meeting that Dudley loved sports—he had come to the meeting wearing his basketball team's jersey and his football team's cap, and his wheelchair had various sports team stickers on it. Using Dudley's interest in sports and the information discussed in the meeting, Ms. Anderson established a work experience at the school district's recreation department, where Dudley was the scorekeeper for the intramural basketball teams. At the same time, Larry worked with Dudley, two of his siblings, and the neighbor who had attended the PCP meeting to identify other sports-related jobs. Two of Dudley's siblings attended the local university, and they connected Larry to the university recreation department manager. Larry conducted an informational interview (see Chapter 5) with the manager and developed a paid internship through the state vocational rehabilitation agency. Dudley later was hired to work in the recreation department at the university.

Box 3.1. Sample Person-Centered Planning Meeting Agenda

Introductions (by Student)

Review of Process

- The focus of PCP is on Dudley's whole life, not just on services or a type of service.

- The plan is Dudley's plan, not the professional's or parents'.

- The people involved in the planning are here at Dudley's (or his parents') invitation.

- There is an emphasis on involving friends and family in the planning; professionals participate to advise, not to control.

- The focus is on a vision for Dudley's future: Practical ways to get there and building commitment not based on compromises with what is but rather based on what can be.

- The emphasis is on Dudley's *strengths, gifts*, and *talents*, building on these and supporting him in areas of current or potential needs, not on a preoccupation with deficits and assessments of "what is wrong with Dudley."

- The challenge is how Dudley, his family, friends, school, and adult services personnel can work together to achieve his vision.

- Dudley's plan may serve as a focus for discussions about what services should be provided, how they can be provided, and who can provide them.

- This process represents a radical shift. It amplifies the voice of Dudley, his family, and his friends.

- This process does not ignore Dudley's disability; it simply shifts the emphasis to a search for capacity in him, among his friends and family, in his community, and among school personnel.

Meeting-Guiding Questions

1. **What is Dudley's history?** (List major milestones, significant events, and things in his life that have impacted or may impact him.)

2. **Who are important people in Dudley's life?** (Include name, relationship, and contact information.)

3. **Who is Dudley as a person?** All members contribute by sharing words/phrases they would use to describe Dudley. There is no right or wrong answer because each person has a different relationship with Dudley. Identify Dudley's unique talents, gifts, strengths, and passions.

4. **What are Dudley's nonnegotiable items?** (List things he must have to be successful, where he likes to go, and what he likes to do.)

   a. What things can make life great for Dudley?

   b. What needs must be met and supports must be in place for Dudley to be successful with his goals?

5. **What is your dream for Dudley as an adult?** (Look beyond the present and dream with him.)

6. **What is your nightmare or concern about Dudley's future?** This is the most difficult question to answer. Identify situations that Dudley and his team should work very hard to avoid, such as things that can ruin Dudley's day.

7. **What would Dudley's ideal day look like now to achieve his vision?** What must be done to make it happen? Who can help? (Include school, employment, recreation, friendships, and home.) **Create an action plan identifying who will do what by when**.

8. **What would Dudley's ideal day look like in 5 years?** What must be done to make it happen? Who can help? (Include school, employment, recreation, friendships, and home.) **Create an action plan identifying who will do what by when. (Forest & Pearpoint, n.d.)**

What is the purpose of education? What is our charge as educators? Education should guide all students and provide them with the skills to become contributing members to society. Whether students continue on to postsecondary education, enter the workforce, join the military, or a combination of these, the ultimate role for school is to prepare young adults for their future life roles. School is a time for students to be provided with experiences that will lead them to careers beyond school. For example, participating in student council may lead to an interest in politics; joining drama club may lead to an interest in the theater or arts; playing on or managing sports teams may build skills in teamwork; working at the school store may lead to an interest in sales or inventory control; and working in the school library may lead to an interest in writing or editing. Students with disabilities need to have these same opportunities to experience activities that can lead to interests in careers once they graduate high school. This chapter addresses how we can plan for employment while students are still in school, can support self-directed meetings, and facilitate adult agency involvement.

PLANNING FOR EMPLOYMENT

Research has consistently shown that young adults who were employed while they were in high school (after school, during the summer) have better postschool outcomes than those who were not employed (Benz, Lindstrom, & Yovanoff, 2000; Carter, Austin, & Trainor, 2012; Carter, Trainor, Cakiroglu, Swedeen, & Owens, 2010; Test, Mazzotti, Mustain, Kortering, & Kohler, 2009). School is an ideal time for students to "try on" job goals and work on the soft skills (e.g., team work, responsibility, dependability, communication, flexibility). The Workforce Innovation and Opportunity Act (WIOA) of 2014 (PL 113-128) requires state vocational rehabilitation agencies to work with students in school to provide Pre-Employment Transition Services (Pre-ETS). These preemployment services have the potential to strengthen the planning process for transition from school to work. There are five Pre-ETS: 1) job exploration, 2) work-based learning experiences, 3) work readiness (or preparation) training, 4) counseling on postsecondary education, and 5) self-advocacy instruction (WINTAC, n.d.). These services can be provided to students who are eligible or potentially eligible for vocational rehabilitation services beginning at age 14. During this time, students should begin to identify areas of interest and areas of need, as well as gain an understanding that all their experiences will help them develop a career path.

While in school, students should also learn the "art" of failure—learning from their mistakes and using the information from past experiences to build their strengths and interests. In order to experience success, students must also experience failure. As students participate in a variety of work and community experiences, not all will be successful, and that is okay. Schools can be a safety net that students may not have in the adult world. As a teacher, you should teach students the art of failure and how students can learn from their mistakes. Making mistakes allows students to learn what they like and do not like, what works and does not work, and to ultimately build their skills toward interdependence.

It is important to view planning and looking for a job with a young adult with a disability the same way you would for yourself. While there may be subtle differences, everything we do in our own job search is individualized just as it is for young adults with disabilities. Some of us find jobs through networking, others apply for positions that are advertised, and still others go to temporary employment agencies to find employment opportunities—there is no one approach that works for everyone. The first step in planning includes building experiences in order to identify strengths, but most importantly, identifying interests and passions. More often than not, students will be unable to articulate their interests and passions, which often makes it seem as though they are not motivated or have no interests. The reality for many students is that they lack exposure to a variety of experiences. For example, at her individualized education program (IEP) meeting, Cambria stated that she was not interested in working. When asked why, she said, "I don't like work." After further discussion, it was discovered that Cambria's in-school work experiences all focused on cleaning: One semester working in the cafeteria cleaning the tables, one semester in the cafeteria sweeping, and one semester in the cafeteria washing dishes. Her view of work was very narrow, and what she was actually saying was that she did not want to work in a cafeteria cleaning. After Cambria was provided work experiences in a variety of settings, she completed a summer internship at a local law firm as a messenger and was ultimately hired after graduation. It is important to understand that exposure to various experiences and opportunities leads to the development of interests that ultimately build motivation (Figure 3.1).

Think about all the experiences you had in and out of school during your middle and high school years. Were you successful in all your experiences? Did you always learn from

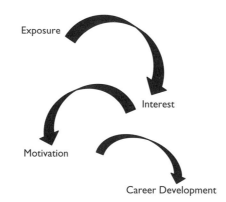

Figure 3.1. Exposure flowchart. (From: TransCen, Inc., Rockville, MD, www.transcen.org; reprinted with permission.)

your mistakes, or did you make similar mistakes over time? If you failed, what happened? Were you told you were not "ready" or that you needed to be more realistic about your career choices? The belief that protecting young adults with disabilities from failing (or sometimes even from trying) can actually be hurting them as they transition to adulthood. Making and learning from mistakes is part of life. As educators, it is important to provide support for young adults not only to succeed but also to learn how to fail.

READY AND RELIABLE

As professionals, we should not be the reality police with students. The idea that someone is not ready for work or is not realistic about his or her job/career path is something we need to work against, as these ideas are killer concepts in moving young adults from school to work. School is a time to explore and experience, a time to succeed and fail. Unless a young adult is putting himself or herself (or others) in danger, any experience should be open for him or her to try. Unfortunately, young adults with disabilities often fall prey to the notion that they are not "ready" for certain experiences or that their ideas about employment are not "realistic." Experiences and opportunities make people ready for work and adult life. Without the opportunity, no one can become ready. Transition professionals must understand that none of our students come to us ready—it is our job to get them ready. Failure is important! Young adults with disabilities need to make mistakes and even fail sometimes in order to learn about what they like and what kind of supports or accommodations they need. Learning occurs from making mistakes.

The view that someone must be ready before he or she can work is a mistake. It is important to remember that no one is "job ready" for any job. Think about your first jobs—were you ready to complete all the job duties up to the standards of the employer on the first day of work? If you really think about it, you learned to be ready through the experience of working. While someone may have the skills or experience to work, employees become ready by working in a business, doing the job. Most newly hired employees are not ready for the job; they become ready by doing the job. Employers understand this, which is why most employers have a probationary period during which employees demonstrate the skills needed for the job and the employer evaluates them on their ability complete the necessary tasks. During the probationary period, new employees learn specific job duties, including productivity and quality requirements, they connect with coworkers, and they learn the culture of the workplace. On occasion, employers may extend an employee's probationary period if the performance is close to expectation but not quite there or if the employee demonstrates a particular skill that is useful to the business. The probationary time is not only for the employer but also for the new employee to determine if the job is a good fit. Self-determination is a critical component during a new employee's probationary period. This is the time for a new employee to ask questions, request accommodations, and develop relationships with coworkers who can provide support and guidance on the job. Sometimes, an employee, once hired, may decide that he or she does not want to work for a particular business or in a specific industry due to the job duties or the workplace culture.

While students are in school, it is important to provide them with opportunities to advocate and evaluate their choices. Unsuccessful experiences can actually lead to a lot of good information about what the student is interested in and what the next steps should be. In addition, young adults should be provided with opportunities to try various jobs in school (e.g., library assistant), participate in activities (e.g., forensics), and volunteer in their community (e.g., local food pantry) so that they can begin to identify what they enjoy doing, what they do not enjoy doing, and why. Consider Lydia's experience.

CASE STUDY Lydia, a young woman who is deaf and blind with some intellectual disabilities and no verbal communication, lived in a state institution for many years and moved to a group home in the community. Because of the perceived severity of her disability and what others viewed as a lack of work-related skills, she was deemed not ready to work. Anne, her former teacher and guardian, wanted her to work. Dwight, her employment consultant, spent time getting to know Lydia and spending time in her community. Her first work experience was in a local hospital near her home where her job duties included stocking the emergency room carts. Lydia demonstrated the skills to complete the job, but each day after about 30 minutes, Lydia became agitated and would begin throwing items and hitting people. It would have been easy for Dwight to determine Lydia not job ready, but instead he spent more time with her and contacted Anne to find out why Lydia might behave this way. Dwight discovered that living in the institution was not a good experience for Lydia, and the hospital emergency room smelled like the institution. Although Lydia had the skills for the job, the work environment was not a good fit. While she was working, Dwight continued to spend time with Lydia in her community, and each Friday they would go to Pizza Hut for lunch. Lydia learned to order her own food using tactile communication symbols, and while Lydia could not verbally communicate, Dwight observed her behaviors. When he observed her in the group home while staff were cooking dinner, Lydia would turn her head toward the kitchen and smile. One day, he worked with Lydia stirring soup on the stove and making Kool-Aid. Lydia smiled, and through her body movements and facial expressions, Dwight discovered that Lydia enjoyed being in the kitchen and around food. After a few months of going to Pizza Hut, the manager asked Dwight about Lydia. He explained that she lived in the area and was looking for a job. He explained that she enjoyed cooking and worked well with her hands. Dwight worked with the manager and developed a job proposal (see Chapter 5). Lydia was hired to make pizza sauce, fold pizza boxes, and put coupons on the boxes. Later, her duties expanded to filling the salad bar using tactile symbols. When Lydia was given a chance to work in the community, she learned the skills needed for that particular business. With her job coach, Lydia increased her productivity during her probationary period and learned duties beyond those she was hired to do. Lydia completed her probationary period and worked at Pizza Hut for 18 years before moving on to another job.

Realistic is another killer concept that can impact a young adult's ability to be successful in working toward his or her employment goals. School is when young adults experience all types of opportunities because school is a time for learning and can be a safety net when young adults are not successful. It is important that educators and family members help young adults through the process of failure because, without failure, there can be no success. Think about the number of times you have failed in your life—and what you learned from those experiences. These same opportunities should be provided to young adults with disabilities. Instead of stating that a young adult's goals are unrealistic, find out *why* he or she is interested in that job or career. Many times, students confuse a "job" with a "company". For example, a student might say he wants to work at Target–Target is a company, not a job. What jobs at Target is he interested in? Why is he interested in those jobs? Does he know someone who works at Target? Does he like wearing the red shirt and name tag? Knowing why a student is interested in a particular job or company is an essential step in assisting him or her in obtaining employment. Renaldo's desire to be a cartoonist illustrates this point.

CASE STUDY   Renaldo wanted to be a cartoonist. While he was a relatively good artist, it would take a long time for him to be able to establish a career as a cartoonist. Instead of telling Renaldo his goals were not realistic, Mr. Edwards, his teacher, got to know him a little better and found out what Renaldo enjoyed about drawing. After spending time talking with Renaldo, Mr. Edwards discovered that he liked drawing because it was a solitary activity (and Renaldo enjoyed being alone), and it was an activity he could do whenever he wanted (Renaldo also liked staying up late at night drawing). After graduation, Renaldo was hired in a mailroom at a large law firm, working second shift (where he worked alone) and did not have to get up early in the morning. He still draws, but as a hobby. And who knows, maybe someday we will see his drawings in a cartoon! But in the meantime, Renaldo is working full time in a mailroom and enjoying his work.

Instead of steering the dream, educators should find out *why* a young adult is interested in a certain job or career and assist in finding experiences that may help lead the person to a successful career path. If a student is interested in sports, assist him or her in participating on a sports team as a player, manager, or keeping statistics; if a student is interested in becoming a rapper or rock star, assist him or her in taking music and poetry classes, participating in a band, or joining a music group. As an educator, you should be the guide on the side rather than the sage on the stage!

Young adults with disabilities should be taught to identify their own employment goals, identify the supports they need, and choose who can help them reach their goals. It is important that the young adult be an active participant and decision maker throughout all aspects of the employment process–from the job search to on-the-job career advancement–as Josh's story illustrates.

CASE STUDY   Josh, a young man with a physical and learning disability, had been employed over the years in multiple dishwashing positions. Over a 2-year period, he had either been fired or quit six different dishwashing positions. When Josh was asked what he wanted to do, he said he wanted to talk on the phone and ask people questions (the employment consultant guessed that he was looking to be a telemarketer). Unfortunately, some of the people around him commented that it was not realistic for Josh to work as a telemarketer due to his physical and learning disability. Josh explained that he did not enjoy dishwashing and wanted to try something different. He worked with an employment consultant who assisted him in finding a job with a local market research company. While Josh required several accommodations to perform some of the job duties (e.g., headset for the phone, voice input computer software, revised information sheet), he worked hard to be successful. He memorized the phone scripts and information and practiced on his own time entering data on his computer. Josh completed his probationary period and was successful for 14 years at his job until he moved to another state. Individuals who exhibit self-determination are typically more successful in their jobs and careers than are those who do not.

How can we begin to plan for employment without focusing on the outdated concepts of "readiness" and "realistic"? One of the most important strategies is self-directed planning.

Students with disabilities should be involved in the planning process through the IEP meetings or through a PCP meeting (which can be part of the IEP meeting). Both the IEP and PCP processes should be led, as much as possible, by the individual and should be viewed as ongoing rather than an end to the process.

EMPLOYMENT FIRST

The key for educators is to ensure students are provided with opportunities to succeed and fail, and to develop self-determination and self-advocacy skills during the process. Employment First (Niemiec, Lavin, & Owens, 2009) practices focus on allowing individuals to make their own choices and learn from those choices. Choice can be a slippery slope. Sometimes, choices offered to individuals with disabilities continue the patterns of segregation, disconnection, and dependency. True informed choice—self-directed choice—includes experiencing life in an array of environments and both succeeding and failing. From these experiences, individuals can begin communicating their beliefs and values to others as well as develop their skills and abilities.

Employment First, simply put, is employment in the general workforce as the first and preferred outcome in the provision of publicly funded services for all working-age citizens with disabilities, regardless of level of disability. It is about raising expectations.

Employment First and self-determination are about opportunity—because skills and interests without opportunity are meaningless. For individuals with disabilities, integrated employment experiences are a means for rehabilitation and an opportunity to provide feedback about those experiences. Individuals with disabilities must be provided with an array of opportunities to experience; communicate their preferences, interests, likes and dislikes; learn from their successes and failures; and maintain high expectations for themselves.

For many years, the special education and rehabilitation literature suggested various methods of PCP. PCP (Hagner, Helm, & Butterworth, 1996; Kincaid, Knabb, & Clark, 2005; O'Brien & Lovett, 1993) methods are value-based approaches for thinking about, communicating with, assessing, planning for, and supporting young adults with disabilities as they move from school to the adult world. Focusing on a student's personal goals and preferences in IEP meetings allows us to satisfy the requirements for team involvement and student choice. As educators, it is important to provide young adults with disabilities opportunities throughout the day that give students 1) the

SELF-DETERMINATION

Self-determination is the freedom to exercise your rights and make choices, the authority to have control over your life, the support to guide you through tough decisions, and the responsibility for determining your future. All people need to develop these skills, but many need help learning how to get started and how to direct their energy productively. Ultimately, self-determination is about service reform: creating a system that allows individuals to make their own choices about what they want to do with their own lives.

PERSON-CENTERED PLANNING

PCP is a process-oriented approach to empowering students with disabilities. It focuses on individuals and their needs by putting them in charge of defining the direction for their lives, not on the systems that may or may not be available to serve them. This ultimately leads to greater inclusion as valued members of both community and society. Among the PCP approaches are Making Action Plans, known as MAPS (Forest & Lusthaus, 1990); Group Action Planning, known as GAP (Turnbull & Turnbull, 1992); Planning Alternative Tomorrows with Hope, known as PATH (Pearpoint, O'Brien, & Forest, 1993); and Essential Lifestyle Planning (Smull, Sanderson, & Allen, 2001).

freedom to have a meaningful life in their school and community; 2) the authority over their current and future earnings; 3) the support to organize resources to reach personal goals; 4) the opportunity to take responsibility for setting goals and a plan to reach them, with support, and 5) the opportunity to gain confirmation of self and to take an active role in decisions about their own life.

WHY IS PERSON-CENTERED PLANNING IMPORTANT?

Obtaining integrated employment requires knowledge of the individual. It is necessary to take a close look at the person's life through a PCP process. PCP provides a foundation of information that is used to individualize job development. PCP is a process of getting to know the individual and facilitating self-discovery and new insight. It is necessary that teachers get to know the student in a variety of environments (home, work, and community settings) and requires spending time with the student instead of simply testing or evaluating him or her. The end goal is to seek a match between the individual's interests/desires and the needs of an employer. Traditional assessment tools typically are used to select or reject vocational services or exclude individuals from the labor market. Often, the findings from these surveys or evaluations determine whether a young adult is job ready. Generally, these assessments are conducted in artificial/simulated settings, and lack reliability and validity data.

PCP is important because it is impossible to find a job match if you do not know who the person is and what he or she is looking for. As with any job search, the student must have control/input in the planning. It is important to understand that the job search process can and will change and that the goal in school is to provide opportunities and experiences from which the young adult can begin to make decisions. By putting the young adult in the driver's seat, you learn more about the individual as she or he learns more about himself or herself—likes and dislikes, types of support that work and types that do not work, and so on. As a result, new and innovative information is gathered (more reliable and less biased) that will lead to successful integrated employment.

PCP allows professionals to get to know the young adult at many different levels: home, community, work, recreation, and relationships with others. This knowledge ultimately leads to increased possibilities for employment and postschool success. PCP is the most basic and effective way of finding out an individual's passions and goals. While it is important to identify areas of need, this must be done within context. Finding out a person's passions is more effective than focusing on a person's deficits. PCP does not ignore disability; it simply shifts the emphasis to a search for capacity in the young adult.

Person-Centered Planning Process

PCP is an art, not a science. As a former job seeker noted, it is a process of providing someone with a compass from which to chart his or her own course of action rather than giving that person a detailed map to follow. The young adult must be included in the planning process and empowered to lead the direction of the meeting by making meaningful choices and informed decisions. It is important to get to know the individual in a variety of settings over a period of time to better understand his or her passions and needs—the young adult must always be the center of the discussion about possibilities (versus what cannot be). PCP has various names, from functional vocational evaluation/assessment to discovery; it is really about community integration and spending time with an individual—hanging out with intent. Because people change on the basis of their experiences, the PCP document will change over time. See Table 3.1 for a sample PCP time line illustrating the planning process.

The first step is for the educator to set up time to visit the student in the home or in an environment outside of school (somewhere in the student's neighborhood) where he or she is comfortable. Before or after the meeting, drive through the immediate neighborhood (about 1-mile radius) noting relevant businesses and organizations. Follow-up meetings should be held in a variety of environments based on student direction (e.g., local library, community center, small room in a coffee shop). Using the observation template (Figure 3.2), spend time with the student in a variety of environments and gather information about a direction for goal setting. While the process is ongoing, it is important to gather as much information as possible to begin to develop a plan of action.

Key skills needed for effective PCP include observation, perception, and checking assumptions. While spending time with the student in various environments, it is important to observe everything, even if you do not think it is important. Sometimes the things you think are unimportant can make the biggest impact on planning, as Rochelle's story illustrates.

CASE STUDY   Rochelle was a young woman participating in a work experience at a local map company. Her job was to tape information into the back of the map books. Each day, she worked hard but her productivity was not where it needed to be. Scott, her job coach, would work alongside Rochelle and she would keep up, but when working on her own, she would slow down. As part of the PCP process, Scott spent some time with Rochelle at her home. Rochelle enjoyed board games and wanted to play Yahtzee! with Scott. As they played, Rochelle would roll the dice, and even though Scott was winning, Rochelle was excited to see her own score get higher with each roll. What Scott discovered was that she did not care whether she won or lost; Rochelle was competitive with herself. On the job, Scott put up tape with Monday to Friday on the wall in Rochelle's work area. Rochelle would stack the books as she completed them; on Monday, she completed 25; on Tuesday she saw how tall the pile was and completed 50; on Wednesday, she beat her Tuesday stack and completed 100. By the end of the week, her productivity was better than the other employees.

Table 3.1.   Person-centered planning process time line

Time	Location	Activity
Week 1	Home visit	Interview family/care providers; observe individual in home environment performing daily living tasks.
Week 2	Community activity	Ask individual what activity he or she would like to participate in (e.g., lunch, library, social activity, exercising).
		Take opportunity to ask additional questions within the context of these activities.
Week 3	Job shadow/work activity	Provide individual an opportunity to shadow several integrated jobs in the community.
Week 4	Job shadow/work activity	Provide individual an opportunity to shadow several integrated jobs in the community.
Week 5	Job shadow/work activity or another community activity	Provide individual an opportunity to shadow several integrated jobs or to be involved in another community activity for additional feedback on the individual's interests and preferences/passions.
	Documentation review	Review related documents for historical and/or medical information after you have established a relationship with individual.
Week 6	Write report	Review your writing to determine that all statements are backed up with observations and nonjudgmental, objective information. Limit amount of hearsay in your report and edit/proofread your report.

Observation Template

Family Information	Sensory
Home Environment	Physical
Medical	Spatial Orientation
Diet	Learning Style/Academics
Financial	Social Skills or Interactions
Transportation	Work History
Communication	Preferences or Choices

Job Interests
Past Work Performance
Strength/Endurance/Hours of Employment
Social Skills
Strengths
Passion/Interests
Communication Skills
Use of Adaptations
Current and Future Support System
Description of Community
Long-Term Employment Goals

Figure 3.2. Observation template.

Perception is another key area to consider when working through the PCP process. Often, our perceptions impact our expectations. Language also plays a big part in our perception about an individual's skills and interests. Look at the information provided about John Doe (Box 3.2).

Box 3.2. Who Is John Doe?

John is an 18-year-old male who has autism.

His behaviors in and out of school are described as violent.

He tried to rip the thermostat off the wall.

He threw the stapler across the room at a worksite.

The behavior strategy used is for John to go to a time-out area in the corner of the room. Often, these time-outs last up to 15 minutes.

According to staff, there are no warnings to his behavioral outbursts.

John is frequently distracted by a preoccupation with objects on the floor.

John often talks loudly at inappropriate times.

He often screams loudly, averaging 12 times per week.

He works at a very slow pace.

He requires one-on-one supervision.

He generally follows directions but is inconsistent.

His Vineland Adaptive Behavior Scales show adaptive skills to be very weak.

John is nonverbal.

John has been successful at keeping his underwear and pants dry during the school day.

John has obsessive-compulsive tendencies; he picks at his face frequently.

What do you think about John? Have you seen information written about your students that focus on deficits? PCP can assist in writing present levels of performance that are balanced, looking at both the deficits and strengths of a student. Take a look at James Doe (Box 3.3).

Box 3.3. Who Is James Doe?

James has a sense of humor and will laugh with you when something is funny.

He has good self-help skills and can take care of himself with hygiene.

He enjoys writing on large sheets of paper.

James enjoys cooking and preparing food for meals.

He lives with his father and enjoys spending time with his mother on Sundays.

James is smart; he can pick up on social cues of others in the room.

He is a perfectionist and is very neat.

James enjoys swimming.

He is perceptive; he knows when people are afraid of him or do not like him.

He loves listening to music.

James likes going out to restaurants.

He keeps his room very neat; everything in its place.

He likes to wear uniforms.

James likes to please others.

He likes to get up early.

He enjoys being active rather than being sedentary or sitting in one place.

James sometimes communicates using one- or two-word phrases.

He picks up on routine very quickly and follows a schedule.

What do you think about James? Could you begin to work with James and identify employment goals? Would it surprise you to know that John and James are the same person? Although extreme, this example shows the power of language: How you talk about a student impacts the perceptions and ultimately the expectations of others. This young adult had strengths *and* areas of need. While it is important to identify areas of need to create supports for the young adult, sometimes these areas of need can change our perceptions about the abilities of the individual. As an educator, it is important to identify the needs in context and begin to develop support strategies. Language and perception often lead to assumptions that may or may not be accurate about the student. Assumptions often lower our expectations about the skills and abilities of young adults. As an educator, it is up to you to ensure that your expectations are lofty for students during the transition planning process. Students will rise to the occasion, and it is up to you to help students through the process of identifying their passions, interests, and skills. As explained earlier, school is a time for students to experience a variety of opportunities so that they can develop goals that will lead them to a fulfilled and meaningful life after high school. Following are examples of the power of language and how perceived deficits can be turned into potential assets.

Stated as a deficit: "Charles has obsessive-compulsive tendencies."

Positive restatement: "Charles is very particular about how books are placed on his bookshelf—all books are in alphabetical order and aligned to the end of the shelf."

Stated as a deficit: "David cannot read material that is given to him."

Positive restatement: "David can recognize letters and numbers and can identify his name and functional and safety words (e.g., stop, exit)."

Stated as a deficit: "Mary is very distractible and has a short attention span."

Positive restatement: "Mary has the ability to multitask and does well at tasks that require 15 to 20 minutes of her time. She is able to complete tasks if she has a sample to check her work against."

The foundations for PCP or hanging out with intent start with attempting to fully understand the student—who the student is, what the student wants, and how you can help the student reach his or her goals. The PCP process is the foundation for developing a summary that the student can take into the adult system once he or she graduates. Activities include interviewing the student and others important in his or her life; observing the young adult in various environments participating in different activities of life and work; reviewing previous records as needed; participating in activities in diverse locations beyond the school setting; involving a variety of people who know the person best and believe in the individual as a future community member—living and working in the community. Gather information to create a positive personal profile (PPP) (see Figure 3.3) of the student and the ideal work environment for him or her. Remember the power of language; be descriptive yet nonevaluative (e.g., Maria is a social, outgoing person = Maria greets people with a "good morning" when she enters a room, smiles, and gives eye contact. Or, Derek hits people = When someone takes an item from Derek without first asking, he holds tight and hits the arm of the person).

You can learn a great deal about your students by prompting them for person-centered information such as the following:

"I like to spend time with _____." (Help students think about family, friends, teachers, neighbors)

"What I did last year was _____." (Often, little things that are important to the person go unnoticed by the team members. People tend to have fewer challenging behaviors when they are doing things they find important and pleasurable.)

Positive Personal Profile

Name: Luciana

Dreams and Goals	**Interests**
Get own apartment with roommate Get a job in retail—likes fashion Learn about finances Learn to become responsible	Color/paint Read Movies—videos and going to movies Cooking Shopping Clothes

Talents, Skills and Knowledge	**Learning Styles**
Singing and dancing Painting and coloring Helping people	Being shown what to do Gets confused if there are too many verbal directions

Values	**Positive Personality Traits**
Church—attends every Sunday and goes to Bible class Family and friends New boyfriend (Jerimiah)	Very talkative Positive outlook Always smiling Always jumping in to help someone

Environmental Preferences	**Dislikes**
None really—wherever I fit in Like quiet places Shift preference starting at 9 but not earlier; prefer not Sunday due to church	Being treated like a child by family

Work Experiences	**Support System**
Grocery store—bagging; didn't like customers getting mad Nursing home—dishes at night; didn't like because people were not friendly Child care—read stories, sanitized toys, fixed food, diapers, etc.; didn't like because got sick and the shift was too early	Case manager—Shana Karl, James, Patricia—teachers and aides

Specific Challenges	**Solutions and Accommodations**
Short temper with other people Gets mad at other people easily	Teaching mindfulness strategies Teaching alternatives to getting mad (e.g, saying excuse me, I'll find someone to help you and walking away)

Career Ideas and Possibilities to Explore
TJ Maxx is near her home and is a place she shops Kohls Dept store—neighbor works there and may be able to connect with manager

Figure 3.3. Sample positive personal profile. (From: TransCen, Inc., Rockville, MD, www.transcen.org; reprinted with permission.)

"During my free time, I like to _____." (Figuring out what a person likes to do can be key to developing new skills.)

"Things that I am good at are _____." (Everyone has talents and gifts. Designing services around strengths allows them to find success in the things they choose to do.)

"To be more independent, I would like to continue working on _____ and learn how to _____." (Strength-based planning allows individuals to use their gifts to meet their own needs.)

"Things that are extremely important to me are _____." (Ask what is important; this gives the student a voice. Professionals tend to focus on "compliance" as opposed to what is important. Breaking down dreams into short-term goals allows for the development of clear plans toward their dreams and away from their nightmares. PCP allows the person to guide the planning process.)

"What community activities will help me to pursue my interests?" (Information should be used to assist students in becoming part of their communities.)

For students with more significant disabilities or who may be nonverbal, using pictures, videos, and direct observations are some ways to gain information. While a student may not be able to verbalize, a lot can be learned from observation. Facial cues, body language, and behaviors (good and bad) can all be indicators of preferences and interests. While it will take longer, the ultimate outcome will be success for the student (review the example of Lydia earlier in the chapter). Sam's transitioning story is an example of how nonverbal communication helped his employment consultant identify his strengths.

CASE STUDY   Sam was a young man who was transitioning from school to work and had difficulty with verbal communication. He spoke one-word "sentences," mumbled to himself, and was extremely shy and fidgety. When spending time with Sam (hanging out with intent to discover his interests), Brittany, his employment consultant, noticed that when they took walks, Sam always wanted to go into the tall buildings downtown and would to take the elevator to the top floor where he would walk around smiling, looking and pointing at the various offices. Sam had no experience in a professional office setting, so Brittany identified a small business that offered Sam an internship. The focus of his internship was on administrative and materials management tasks, and he learned a great deal, including the phrase "Ladies first" as he held the elevator or door for others. During the internship, Brittany observed Sam and his body language and facial expressions. Sam was always smiling and was engaged in learning the new administrative tasks. Toward the end of his internship, Sam had developed his skills in sorting, organizing, and filing tasks. His speed and accuracy impressed his supervisor at the business, and one of his coworkers called Sam a "filing machine." Focusing on Sam's strengths, Brittany approached a large and busy law firm to evaluate its needs and developed a job proposal for a part-time office clerk position to manage the day-to-day office needs. The HR director agreed to a hands-on interview in the firm's file room. Sam saw a file that was misfiled and fixed it immediately. He then held the door to the HR director's office and said, "Ladies first," as everyone was leaving. The HR director said that others in the office could learn something from Sam and suggested they hire him as a part-time office clerk. Later, he was asked to work with some of the firm's lawyers on an appeals case. There were many files to maintain from the original trial, and the lawyers needed Sam's help to organize the trial documents. Sam increased his skills and is now working with the accounting and HR departments, assisting the paralegals, and working on various cases organizing files for the lawyers.

Person-Centered Planning Meeting

The next step in the planning process is to conduct a PCP meeting. The first step is to generate a list of people to invite to the meeting; talk with the student and conduct a relationship map to identify the people who are important in the student's life. Initially, the student may not know who to invite, but later, this will be an easier process. Possible attendees could include neighbors, school or work friends, school personnel, and family members. It is important to balance the number of professionals with nonprofessionals so that the meeting does not turn into a typical school meeting. The educator will then work with the student to develop and send personalized invitations. It is important to keep this activity age appropriate (e.g., using a computer or creating something in art class). Once the invitations are designed and developed, assist the student in sending out the invitations via e-mail or mail or in person.

The initial meeting should take place outside of the school whenever possible, somewhere in the community or at the student's home. During the meeting, the teacher can serve as the facilitator, assisting the student to introduce the attendees and how they are connected to his or her life. The educator and student can decide which questions or format to use for the meeting.

The emphasis of PCP is to focus on the student's interests and preferences: What kind of work is the student interested in doing? What type of work at home or in the community has the student done in the past? What are the family's work expectations? What are the student's existing skills and support needs? What support does the student use now? How does the student learn new skills? What teaching strategies seem to work best? Person-centered planning is like a first date, a personal way to get to know who a person is right now and helps you see a better opportunity for growth. Echoing the famous words of Forrest Gump, person-centered planning "is like a box of chocolates, you never know what you're gonna get" (Zemeckis, 1994).

USEFUL RESOURCES

The *Social Security Redbook* is a great tool to answer questions about benefits and work incentives: https://www.ssa .gov/redbook

Work Incentive Issue Brief: https://www.ssa.gov/ disabilityresearch/documents/ WIPA%20brief_final010312 .pdf

Ticket to Work information: https://www.ssa.gov/work

Local WIPA: https://choosework .ssa.gov/findhelp/

Utilizing Person-Centered Planning Information

After the PCP meeting is complete, the facilitator or educator compiles the information from the meeting and summarizes it to include the student's goals, the action steps to help the student move to the next phase, who will assist the student moving forward, and a time line. Assist the student in maintaining the time line and develop a work plan to achieve his or her goals. Transition activities that result from the PCP can then be focused on Pre-ETS and incorporated into the student's IEP. Activities could include 1) job exploration (e.g., career fairs, career days, and visits from local community members sharing career experiences); 2) work-based learning that includes job shadowing (the student follows an employee during a typical day on the job), mentoring (the student is matched with an adult mentor in a specific business or industry), workplace tours (the student observes different work settings and conducts an informational interview to research that career path), internships (paid or unpaid work experience for students), volunteering (donating time to work in a local nonprofit organization such as a nursing home or food bank), afterschool and summer jobs arranged and supported by school staff, apprenticeship (an adult professional teaches the student a specific trade), service learning (classroom instruction paired with community service, such as working with Habitat for Humanity or other organizations, to teach civic responsibility and strengthen communities); 3) counseling on postsecondary education options (community college enrollment as a high school student–dual enrollment can ease the transition to postsecondary education and can help the student become part of his or her community); 4) workplace readiness (mock job interviews and job clubs with fellow students, training in financial literacy, mobility training, Skills to Pay the Bills curriculum, social and problem-solving skills training); 5) self-advocacy instruction (peer mentoring, goal setting, understanding and requesting accommodations, problem solving, knowing rights and responsibilities under the Americans with Disabilities Act [ADA] and WIOA) (WINTAC, n.d.).

Providing students with experiences to learn about different job and career options is critical in transition planning. Financial literacy is an important component to workplace readiness. Too often, the message to young adults with disabilities and their families is to not work or to work just enough to avoid impacting their benefits (e.g., Supplemental Security Income). Understanding work the impact on benefits is essential during transition planning, and the discussion must occur often so that there is a clear understanding.

Benefits Planning

The Work Incentive Planning and Assistance (WIPA) program was established by the Social Security Administration to provide all Social Security Disability Income (SSDI) and Supplemental Security Income (SSI) disability beneficiaries (including transition-to-work-age youth) with free access to work incentive planning and assistance. If the student receives SSDI or SSI benefits, it will be important to contact a community work incentive coordinator (CWIC). CWICs are specially trained counselors to assist SSI and SSDI recipients in making informed choices about working. The Social Security Administration has many work incentives, so the question no longer has to be "Can I work?" but should be "How can I work?" In school, educators should be aware of the Student Earned Income Exclusion. This provision allows a student who is under age 22 and regularly attending school to exclude earnings from income. "Regularly attending school" means that the person takes one or more courses of study and attends classes in a college or university, for at least 8 hours a week; or in grades 7–12, for at least 12 hours a week; or in a training course to prepare for employment, for at least 12 hours a week (15 hours a week if the course involves shop practice); or in a home school situation, for at least 12 hours per week and in accordance with the home school law of the state or jurisdiction in which the student resides. Other work incentives that could assist students as they transition to work include an Impairment-Related Work Expense (IRWE) and a Plan for Achieving Self-Support (PASS). Educators should have information about Social Security work incentives and connect with work incentive counselors in their area. Ideally, students should leave with a benefits analysis prior to graduation so that they understand how work will impact their benefits. The bottom line is that students can work and should be encouraged to work, and benefits should not be a barrier to employment. While you do not need to be an expert in Social Security work incentives, it is important to have information to share with young adults and their families. The *Social Security Red Book* (2018) is a helpful guide if you cannot find a benefits-planning specialist in your area.

Finding the Right Adult Services Agency

Locating an adult services agency can be a difficult and confusing task, especially if you have never had any experience in finding and setting up services. A good first place to start is to contact your state vocational rehabilitation or developmental disabilities agency. Many states have "macro teams" such as transition advisory groups or other transition-focused assemblages that bring adult agencies and schools together.

Having a representative present to your class or work with the student to schedule a meeting with a vocational rehabilitation representative will allow educators to obtain information about other adult services organizations in the area. Not all employment service programs are alike; they vary in size, types and variety of services offered, qualifications of staff, range of people served, and most important, quality of results. An assignment for students during their transition years can be to identify and research adult services agencies that they would like to work with once they leave school. Several of the Common Core standards relate to research and writing. Transition planning can be embedded in the standards set for all students. Asking the right questions (Figure 3.4) of adult services agency representatives is critical. Exploring employment programs in your area will give you information on the services and related resources available as well as a sense of which provider is the best match for your students. When shopping around for an employment service provider, be sure to inquire whether the provider has current openings well suited to your student and, if not, approximately how long it will be before an opening becomes available. It is important that the organization with which you collaborate has the same high expectations for your students as you do.

Preparation for work and collaboration with agencies improves the likelihood that students will move into employment and careers after high school; students with even the most difficult challenges have demonstrated that they can be successful moving from school to work or to more education. Further, young adults with disabilities who pursue advanced education and/or job training ultimately exercise some control over job choice rather than simply taking any job. It is critical that schools help young adults get ready for employment by setting expectations and providing career preparation and work experiences.

Deciding on Employment Options

Employment is generally defined as either competitive or supported, using customized strategies. Competitive employment means working in a job found in your local community with or without the assistance of an adult services provider. What makes these jobs competitive is that you must compete with others to fill job openings. Employees in these jobs are paid wages and receive benefits (health/dental insurance, vacation) typical for that type of job. For example, a local grocery store is looking for utility clerks. A young adult with a disability could apply and interview for the job, with or without the support of a job coach. The employer hires the student at the same wage as other utility clerks hired.

Supported employment using customized strategies is useful for students with more significant disabilities and means working in a job found in your local community with the assistance of an adult services provider. Jobs are found according to the interests and abilities of the young adult and are negotiated according to the needs of the business by the adult services provider. Customized strategies focus on the assets and strengths the job seeker can bring to the business. Job tasks are reassigned from an existing job, restructured from one or more existing jobs, or created to match the skills and accommodation needs of the job seeker and must help the employer's operation in some specific way. Customized employment strategies focus on the value a job seeker can bring to the business. When tasks are reassigned to customize a job, it is not done in a way that points out what the job seeker cannot do; rather, it emphasizes what the person can do that will bring value to the business. Support through a job coach or coworker is provided to help the new employee keep the job or move into

Questions to Ask Supported Employment Providers

1. What are the eligibility requirements for services?
2. How do I apply for services?
3. Does your agency have a waiting list? If yes, how long?
4. What services do you provide?

a.	Assessment	Yes	No
b.	Job development	Yes	No
c.	Job support	Yes	No
d.	Training classes	Yes	No

       i.   Specify type(s) _____

       ii. Are they group classes?

       iii. Are they individual classes?

e.	Transportation	Yes	No

       i.   Type of transportation:

f.	Community Recreation	Yes	No
g.	Community Access	Yes	No
h.	Advocacy	Yes	No

      i. Other _____

5. Are your services time-limited? Please explain.
6. Are there ways that your agency and local schools can work together to ensure a smooth transition?
7. If I need job accommodations or assistive technology, do you provide these services?
8. If I graduate with a job, would it be easier to provide services than if I still need support to find and learn a job?
9. How many staff work in your agency?

   a. How many clients does each staff member have?
10. What if I lose my job? Will I stay with your agency?
11. How long does it generally take to assist someone in getting a job?
12. What is the average pay for clients who get jobs through your agency?
13. What is the retention rate in jobs for clients who get jobs through your agency?
14. Does your agency work with anyone interested in working, regardless of his/her disability?
15. Does your agency provide support after before 9 a.m. and after 5 p.m.? On weekends?
16. Does your agency find permanent jobs in the community?
17. How does your agency determine what a good job is for clients?
18. How does your agency terminate services?
19. Does your agency provide benefits counseling (if I receive SSI or SSDI)?
20. Does your agency look at advancement in jobs beyond entry-level work?
21. How do you obtain input and maintain communication with the client and family members?
22. Can I get a tour of your agency?
23. Can I talk with some individuals with disabilities who have used your services?
24. Do you have literature?

    a. Brochure

    b. Web site

    c. Other literature

Figure 3.4. Questions to ask supported employment providers. (From Wisconsin Department of Public Instruction, *Opening Doors to Employment,* Bulletin 09012, © 2008, https://www.witc.edu/sites/default/files/inline-files/Opening-Doors-Transitional-Guide%5B1%5D.pdf. Adapted by permission.)

other positions in that business. Supports and services are designed on the basis of the needs of the young adult. Employees in these jobs are paid wages by the employer and may receive benefits (health/dental insurance, vacation). For example, Dan is looking for a job but has limited verbal skills and has never worked before. An adult services provider meets with local businesses in Dan's community to find out their needs and determine a match between Dan's interests and skills and the needs of the business. Together, the adult services provider and employer identify four or five tasks that need to get done but often do not get done because employees are doing other duties. The adult services provider negotiates a part-time position for Dan to complete these four or five tasks. While on the job, the job coach will work with Dan to increase his skills and identify additional tasks he is able to complete for the business, adding more value as an employee.

Self-employment and entrepreneurship represent another employment option, especially for, but not limited to, individuals who live in rural communities where employment opportunities may be limited. Self-employment customizes employment opportunities so individuals can create a work environment optimizing the flexibility and accommodations they may need. Self-employment should not be a hobby job at which someone might make a small amount of money per year but rather a viable, self-sustaining employment option for an individual whereby the business is established for the individual to ultimately support himself or herself. Certainly a hobby job could supplement another job the individual has. There are many resources available for individuals interested in self-employment, and it is important to keep in mind that this option is not for everyone.

When individuals with a disability own, manage, and/or operate their own business to earn money, there are many benefits, such as independence and the opportunity to make their own business decisions, the ability to set their own pace and schedule, reduction of transportation issues if the business is home based, and continued support from Social Security through work incentives such as PASS. If self-employment is of interest, it is important to connect with other organizations (i.e., vocational rehabilitation) and identify possible funding and planning support.

An example of sustainable self-employment is Poppin Joe's Kettle Korn. Poppin Joe's Gourmet Kettle Korn was officially launched in April 2005 with Joe Steffy, a young man with Down syndrome and autism spectrum disorder, as the sole proprietor. After Joe graduated high school, his parents were told that Joe would never be able to hold down a job. Fortunately for Joe, his parents had high expectations and were determined to show that he could work. Joe and his father began popping kettle corn on weekends at grocery stores around their community. Joe learned the process for making kettle corn and was able to stay on task for up to 6 hours. His mother helped write a business plan, and the Kansas Department for Developmental Disabilities awarded Joe a grant to purchase his equipment. Joe's business continues to grow each year, and he has sales of around $75,000 annually. Operating and managing his own business, Joe has developed a strong work ethic and is a productive member of the community.

As an educator, your goal is to maintain high expectations to prepare students for competitive integrated employment. It will be important to reach out to your state vocational rehabilitation system to collaborate on Pre-ETS once a student turns 14. For some students, work experiences can start out within the school, such as working in the library, assisting in the office, delivering mail within the building, or working in the school store or school business (e.g., coffee shop). Later, students might volunteer at a local food/clothing bank, help deliver meals to the elderly, or be guest readers to a local child care facility in the community. In-school and out-of-school businesses can also be developed, such as a school coffee shop or a lawncare/snow removal business for the neighborhood surrounding the school.

While providing work experiences during school, it might be appropriate to provide employment experiences using a model in which two to three students participate in a work experience within the same business. For example, in a hospital setting, one student could work in the laundry, one student could work in central supply, and one student could work in medical records, with one adult supporting all three students within that business and utilizing natural supports.

Adult Service Provider Vignette

Mr. Burns is working with Cameron, a young man with mental health issues. Cameron has difficulty maintaining focus due to auditory hallucinations and additional mental health issues. Mr. Burns worked with Cameron to identify individuals to invite to a PCP meeting. Mr. Burns explained that the meeting would help explore Cameron's strengths, areas of need, and interests and would identify an action plan with a time line and supports. He explained that there might be some uncomfortable discussions about Cameron's behavior but that everyone there wanted to help him be successful. Cameron had a difficult time identifying people to invite other than his sister and mother. He said he had no friends and did not know who else to invite. After spending some time with Cameron, observing what he did while he was at home and school, Mr. Burns helped Cameron identify his neighbor and his history teacher as additional people to invite. Mr. Burns worked with Cameron to develop a date, time, and location for this meeting. Cameron created personalized invitations on the computer and wanted to have his picture on the invitation. Cameron gave each person the invitation. At the meeting, Cameron's neighbors, an elderly couple, indicated that he would come over to help with the laundry and do lawn work and that he would even explain television shows to them. This was a surprise to his mother, as he did not do those chores at home. During the meeting, Cameron's interests in history, helping people, and fixing bicycles were identified. Several ideas were discussed, such as working in an independent living center (where he could talk about historical events with the residents), working at the local historical society, or working in a bicycle shop. Each member of the team had contacts or ideas to get a connection with each of these types of businesses. Cameron started out as in intern transporter in a local nursing home identified by his history teacher. The experience was not what Cameron had hoped. His next experience was identified by his neighbor who knew the owner of a local bicycle repair shop. After a work-based learning experience, the owner hired Cameron to put bikes together and assist in repairs.

➡ TIP   As an educator, answer the following questions: 1) Do I encourage my students to make choices and decisions on a day-to-day basis? 2) Do I honor the choices and decisions that my students make? 3) Do I actively involve my students in their own IEP meetings/conferences? 4) Do I include self-determination goals in my students' IEPs? 5) Do I know how to measure progress on self-determination goals?

It is important to remember these points:

PCP is not a single event; it is ongoing.
Observations should be inclusive of people, places, and things.
Discovery should be person centered and person directed.
A functional analysis always occurs in authentic locations.

SUMMARY

PCP is a critical component in transition and aligns with the individualized planning provided through the IEP. Every student has different needs, goals, skills, and preferences. By getting to know each student in multiple settings; creating opportunities for the student to try out jobs through volunteering, internships, or paid employment; and working with the student and his or her family to better understand how work may impact Social Security and other benefits, you can help ensure students will have a successful transition to the adult world.

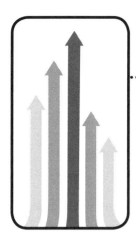

4

Developing Skills, Identifying Passions, and Exploring Careers

Ms. Spencer is a transition coordinator for the program serving students ages 18–21 at a large rural high school. Her program involves a variety of experiences for her students, including a school-based entrepreneurial cookie business, community-based work experiences, and inclusion in general curriculum academic and related activities. A student named Judy was referred to her with the following information from her high school teacher: "Judy is an 18-year-old student with Down syndrome. She is nonverbal, has behavioral issues requiring a one-on-one aide at all times, should remain in a self-contained classroom learning basic self-care skills, and is best suited for a sheltered workshop or day service placement upon exiting school." Ms. Spencer was surprised at the low expectations and negative portrayal of Judy and decided to find out for herself who Judy was and what she was most interested in.

She arranged for Judy to work in the school cookie business and to join others in activities such as decorating for pep club rallies. Interestingly, she started to learn a very different side of Judy. Ms. Spencer noticed that Judy did not like using the augmentative speech device but could demonstrate with sounds and gestures the message she was trying to get across. She noticed that other students were able to understand Judy and enjoyed her sense of humor. Because of Judy's interest in the cookie business, Ms. Spencer arranged for Judy to complete a community-based work experience with a local coffee and baked goods shop, where she was responsible for replenishing and arranging the condiments. The coworkers and customers loved Judy and would seek her out to engage in interactions with her. Ms. Spencer saw a decrease in negative behaviors to the point that they were almost nonexistent. It seemed that Judy had exhibited these behaviors in the past over her frustration with not being understood and with being ignored in communication. The more she had behaved in ways that were negative, the more she was pulled from the other students and the activities she most enjoyed.

Ms. Spencer identified the ways of communicating that Judy preferred and established goals for Judy that would help her indicate those preferences to others and respond in ways that were more constructive than her past behaviors. Her school program included additional opportunities in the community where Judy's true passions could be determined and where she could learn from others. The methods of communication, the trigger points, and the response patterns were summarized in her current level of performance along with a description of Judy's personality, desire to be involved with her peers, and interest in work. Her goals to learn how to communicate with and respond to others, to develop alternative behaviors when frustrated, to further expand her work skills, and to identify the type of jobs and environmental characteristics she liked most became her IEP goals to be addressed through additional and varied employment experiences over her remaining school years.

The goal of education is for all students to achieve their postsecondary education and/or employment goals when they graduate. It is sometimes challenging as an educator to ensure that the activities you are completing will contribute toward these postschool outcomes. Several key principles can help guide this process. First, having high expectations for all students, including those with disabilities regardless of the level of severity, and providing them with the opportunities that prepare them for work lays a valuable foundation. Second, purposefully engaging all youth so they become equipped with the knowledge and skills to express their preferences and support needs to others both within and outside of school is a critical element. Finally, gaining an understanding of and including the business community and adult service delivery systems enhances the relevance and connectivity of the student's educational experience with his or her desired postschool life.

Interestingly, many of the factors that contribute to success for students with disabilities are the same as those for students without disabilities, such as their education program, instructional quality, and access to mentors (National Technical Assistance Center on Transition [NTACT], 2018). Additional elements that we know contribute to the postschool employment outcomes for students with disabilities include paid work experience, vocational training, career development, inclusion in general curriculum, development of self-advocacy skills, and parent expectations (NTACT, 2018). A complete listing of postschool indicators contributing to postschool outcomes can be located at https://transitionta.org. Regardless of your role, it is important to focus your efforts on these common practices. Never underestimate the impact you can make or how powerful a single message, activity, or connection can be for a student. Being a role model, displaying your passion, and demonstrating confidence in everything you do will go a long way toward instilling similar attributes in the students you encounter.

School is the time to explore opportunities and provide students with experiences that assist them with making choices about what they want to do when they graduate. Emphasis should be placed on trying new things, being exposed to different environments, and expanding the possibilities from which to choose. Providing an array of activities offers tremendous variation in assessment information to help determine instructional plans and get to know the student best. Think about the benefits of discovering what a student likes and does not like, what he or she is good at, the kinds of supports that are needed and helpful, and the many talents the student has to offer, all of which contribute to a good job match and successful employment. Equally important is "packaging" this information and communicating it with others to positively influence the expectations and decision making of those impacting employment.

DEVELOPING HIGH SCHOOL SERVICES

Regardless of where the student is in the transition process, it is essential that efforts start with the end goals in mind and be gauged in relation to their contributions for achieving an inclusive and quality adult life. Driven by what the student and family want, it is important to determine their dreams and hopes for the future. Families may convey these dreams and hopes generally, such as having a job and living independently, or more specifically, such as obtaining a career in the legal field.

As members of the team, teachers can use this information to guide their educational instruction and experiences to assist the student with achieving these desired postschool outcomes as well as advocating with other school and adult services personnel to inform and engage their support.

For example, Sarina was a high school student with a cognitive disability and seizure disorder resulting in more than 100 seizures per day. The school felt that Sarina's seizures posed a risk for her to be in the community and, for her safety, felt that preparing for adult life that included employment and independent living would never happen. As a result, her school program was limited to in-building activities that were not stressful and did not challenge Sarina to learn and grow. Her parents raised issues at her IEP meeting stating that they expected Sarina to have her own apartment and a job when she graduated. They indicated her level of independence at home and how they were working to teach Sarina how to know when she was going to have a seizure, how to ask for help, and how to manage them for herself and those around her after they occurred. They requested the same considerations be included in her school programming.

As a result, Sarina's IEP goals were expanded to include community-based work experiences where she was taught to handle her seizures in those environments, explaining to others what she needed and learning to manage them on her own. Thus, Sarina's educational program became guided by the end goal of employment and the steps to get there as opposed to the developmental model of ensuring her seizures were in check before additional opportunities were provided. What often occurs with the latter way of thinking is that students like Sarina may never meet the readiness criteria established, such as having her seizures controlled, and consequently leave school without ever receiving the training and support to achieve their postschool goals. An alternative and effective approach is to recognize that Sarina has seizures and include functioning within those parameters as part of the end goal and the steps to get there.

Finding out the requirements needed to be successful in those expanded environments, establishing the student's current level of performance in each of those challenging areas, and identifying the discrepancies for instruction begins the roadmap for bridging the gap between the two. The assessment process identified in this chapter contributes to the description of the student's current level of performance, laying the foundation for the development of instructional goals to bring the student closer to achieving his or her postschool goals. The broad steps are reflected in the student's annual IEP goals, which are broken down into specific objectives outlining the activities for achieving them. Revisiting the goals annually allows for adjustments in the roadmap to prevent "getting stuck" in any one particular area. While the plan may be for a student to learn a skill, it is important to remember that teaching for independence is the first step; there may be ways to modify the task to do it differently or build in supports to enable the student to be able to complete or partially complete it. This is also a good time to determine if there are any changes in the student's goals and to verify that the steps targeted for each year are in line for moving the student closer to his or her goals in the remaining time period before graduation.

All too often, these options are limited by what someone feels the student can do or what is perceived as being available to them. For example, David was given the task of shredding documents at his school because it was felt this was the only job he was able to do. He completed this task in the school office for an hour a day, 3 days a week, through all 4 years of high school. David was able to put the piece of paper in the shredder and was considered successful for completing this single task. Learning more about what a job in this area would require, working at a competitive rate, learning problem solving (e.g., when the paper got jammed), asking for more work, socially interacting with others were never included as part of David's work experience. Consequently, he was referred to adult services with the limited description that all he could do was the single task of shredding paper, and no other vocational information was provided to contribute to his employment goal. Concerns were raised as to whether David could work competitively, and ultimately, it was decided that he would attend the sheltered workshop to learn the skills he needed to be employable. Unfortunately, there is clear and compelling evidence that this path is unlikely to lead to employment for David or the many other young adults who exit school to attend sheltered work and day programs (Nazarov, Golden, & von Schrader, 2012; Wehman, 2009). So, what can be done differently during the school years to turn this outcome around?

Let's explore the following example: Jessica and her parents indicated they wanted competitive employment as the outcome when Jessica graduated from high school. At the beginning of ninth grade, Jessica stated that she did not know what she wanted to do. Her teacher arranged for Jessica to have six different work experiences that year in a variety of community businesses exposing her to many types of jobs and work environments. Jessica expressed interest working in settings involving office work, animals, and people. The next year, Jessica's teacher arranged for her to have three work experiences and several job shadowing opportunities so she could begin to explore which areas she enjoyed the most and the environmental characteristics that are so critical, such as loud or quiet, crowded or working alone, fast paced or slow paced.

The teacher communicated the assessment information from those experiences to Jessica's 11th-grade teacher, who identified two different work experiences in businesses involving office tasks with very different environments, one of which was technology-oriented, as Jessica had shown some interest at one of the sites she had visited. Jessica participated at a community-based work experience at both of these jobs during the school year. The duties she learned and the quality and rate at which she completed them were the same as what was expected of anyone working in those positions. The teacher provided instruction, implemented technology and other compensatory strategies, and modified how the task was completed on the basis of training data.

In addition, Jessica had opportunities to learn how to communicate directly with the company supervisor and to interact socially with other coworkers. By her senior year, Jessica's teacher had a good idea of what Jessica liked, what she wanted to do, how she learned best, and areas of support that would be critical for her success. A work experience for 4 hours a day, 4 days a week was identified on the basis of these factors. Jessica worked in an office and learned the many tasks required as well as the work-related behaviors that were expected of her. She developed friendships and connections that would later be valuable contacts for permanent employment. Further, Jessica had built an impressive resume over her high school years highlighting her skills and accomplishments. Most important, Jessica was referred to adult services where she articulated what type of job she would like and the characteristics that were important to her; she also provided comprehensive assessment information that would help them find a job for her and support her in employment. As a result, Jessica was referred for supported employment services with the competitive employment goal of a full-time office position. Jessica and David had very different outcomes despite that they presented themselves similarly when they entered high school, varying only in the 4-year educational programming that followed.

It is important to revisit why vocational training is such an integral part of a student's overall education experience. For many students who never have the opportunity to experience afterschool and summer employment, exposure to work while in high school is the only chance they have to learn real-world labor market demands. Additionally, these experiences contribute to promoting a work ethic, a critical element in any employment situation and greatly valued by the business community.

Their peers are involved with work, which provides a platform of shared experiences that equalizes communication and social relationships. Consider the limitations of not participating in a variety of work experiences and how difficult it would be to respond to questions asking what you want to do after you graduate. Many students answer with all they know: what they watch on TV, fastfood restaurants they eat at, department stores they shop at, and conversations they hear others having. For example, one 21-year-old student responded to the question "What do you want to do when you leave school?" with a smile and answered, "Be a volunteer." It is evident she heard those words from someone else, as it can be argued very few people complete their education with aspirations for the career goal of becoming a volunteer. She was unable to describe what that would be, and the IEP team determined she would go into a volunteer situation because "that was her choice."

When these responses alone are considered an individual's employment goal and he or she is earmarked to enter these vocations prematurely and without the opportunity to try out different vocational situations and make an informed choice, the irreplaceable richness of experience is lost. Equally critical is finding out students' passions and what they show an interest in, what excites them, and what they like to do, all of which contributes to a well-matched employment goal. The school years offer opportunities for exploring these avenues that are often not readily available within adult services primarily because of the differences in services between the two in terms of eligibility, funding, staffing, and accountability. The more students can gain these opportunities while in school, the greater their chance for post-secondary education or employment when they graduate (Test, Mazzotti, Mustain, Kortering, & Kohler, 2009; Wehman, 2009). Rather than checking off that a vocational goal was determined, the essential element is exploring the qualitative aspects of what that means for the student and his or her preferences, including an employment goal, characteristics, and work environments.

IDENTIFYING LEARNING STYLES AND PREFERENCES

When we think about school years as a period of exploration, many of the activities the student participates in take on a new emphasis. Using opportunities within the regular school day to observe the student and get an idea of his or her skills, interests, support needs, and instructional resources can be a valuable component of the assessment process. Opening our eyes objectively to the factors potentially impacting an individual's employment can help us avoid overlooking an important variable that we may attribute to the wrong cause.

For example, if a student has a behavioral outburst when entering math class, we may assume that the student does not like math, but on closer scrutiny, we may discover the reaction has an environmental trigger, such as the temperature, layout, building location, the teacher's style, other students, a need for more or different supports, the response the student experiences, or a sign of frustration. Capturing the information objectively allows us to paint a picture over time of what may or may not be important for the student, particularly if the student cannot communicate his or her feelings directly. Documenting a description of the environment and events leading to the outburst and those that happen afterward can help us see what other contributing factors may be at play. Interestingly, this same student who was perceived as disliking math in 10th grade reported it was his favorite class in his junior year. Often, we jump to the wrong conclusions when we look at the situation too broadly or rely on our subjective interpretation of what appears to be the obvious.

For many students, observation and reports from others who know the student well are the most valuable techniques for learning more about the individual. Observing the student perform and participate in a variety of settings and activities is very useful in order to paint the big picture as well as begin distinguishing variations across people, places, and events.

One of the most informative activities is participation in a real work situation in a community business. Several options are available for gathering this assessment information through career exploration activities. One option is to arrange job shadowing opportunities where students can visit a business and walk through the workday with an experienced worker, providing them the opportunity to learn firsthand about the position and the work environment. While this does not provide direct hands-on experience, valuable insight into the specific aspects of the job and their appeal to the student can be gleaned.

In addition, types of jobs and, more important, different settings within certain categories of work can be determined. For example, a student who enjoyed music was taken to a chain technology store where he turned around and walked out saying he did not want to work there. School personnel took him to a locally owned trendy music shop, and the student ran right up to the counter and asked if he could have a job. What were the differences? Both businesses were in the area of music, but at the first store, the setting was large and bright; pop music played through the speakers; and most of the salespeople were middle age and dressed in suits. In contrast, the second setting was small and dark with colorful lights, hip hop and rock music were played, and the salespeople were in their late teens to early 20s and dressed in jeans.

Often, when students tell us the type of job they would like to work in, such as working with computers, it is easy to jump to a specific job in that category, forgetting that each environment of even the same kind of business can be very different. Job shadowing can provide a wealth of information to help determine job preferences for additional in-depth exploration. The Job Observation Assessment Form (Figure 4.1) provides a useful tool for students to be able to express their preferences about the critical components of the job, including the workplace, people, and job duties for each of the businesses they visit.

A second option is to conduct situational assessments involving 3- to 4-hour work assessments in three different community businesses reflective of the types of jobs that exist in a community and present varied environments, tasks, and social situations for the student to try. The purpose of a situational assessment is to observe in a variety of settings in order to find out different aspects of a job that the individual likes and dislikes (e.g., indoor or outdoor, fast or slow paced), how he or she learns best (e.g., verbal prompts or modeling), specific work skills and interests (e.g., mail delivery, cleaning, computers), social interactions and getting along with others (e.g., supervision, coworker preferences), support needs (e.g., orienting, telling time, sequencing tasks), and personal attributes (e.g., strength, speed, time of day). This is also a good time to try strategies that were found effective in the classroom related to stress or behavioral issues, such as meltdowns, refusal to work, or anger outbursts, and assess their application in a community work setting.

One suggestion for arranging situational assessments is to contact businesses to set up long-term ongoing assessment sites. (*Note:* If an employer is interested in hiring a student, say yes! Ultimately, this is what you want for your students. Often, teachers assume that these businesses are the school's sites. If an employer hires a student, then simply look for another business to provide a place for assessments.) Think about the type of industries in the local community and then visit some to learn about their willingness to have students brought in during the school year to conduct assessments. Finding out the specifics of the company and the tasks to be performed, the attire to be worn, and rules to follow and documenting this information for future assessments will prevent the burden of repeating these requirements each time. It is a good idea to make arrangements with about 8–10 businesses that offer a variety of opportunities. Required paperwork can be completed to formalize the specifics of the arrangement, such as responsibilities and liability.

Job Observation Assessment Form

Name: _____   Job location: _____

	Liked 😊	OK 😐	Didn't Like ☹️	Would you like to work here?
The Workplace				Yes 👍 No 👎
The People				
The Job Duties				
Overall Job				Comments

Figure 4.1. Job observation assessment form.

While the jobs performed as part of assessment are not necessarily what the student is going to want to do, the experience will help identify certain positive aspects of the job that will contribute to making a good job match. A good job match combines the individual's passions with those positive aspects of real workday activities. Generic sites are likely to be used for scheduling assessments for students; however, there are times that exceptions within a specific business will be considered to gain more detailed information about an individual's skills or interests in a particular field, such as a lumber yard, funeral home, or child care facility. Recording information on the Situational Assessment Form can provide a useful description across a variety of experiences (Figure 4.2). A useful tool to assist with recording and synthesizing work assessment observations is shown in Figure 4.3.

A narrative summary can be helpful to synthesize what has been gathered and capture your insights and interpretations for moving forward. Sharing these tools with adult services such as vocational rehabilitation and community support providers will greatly contribute to the employment process and is often the only source for receiving this important information.

UTILIZING ONLINE CAREER EXPLORATION TOOLS

Students often spend a great deal of time on the computer. Why not use this handy resource as a means for conducting career exploration activities? Computerized curricula and interest inventories can be accessed universally, and they allow for self-directed, self-paced learning. At the same time students are learning content, they are being exposed to skills development in using technology. Teachers often report an ease in utilizing computerized instructional materials, as they allow for flexibility in teaching and provide individualized supports. Most important, they are appealing and motivating to youth and level the playing field for them with their transition-age peers. Some examples of online sites for career exploration include the following:

Mapping Your Future (https://www.mappingyourfuture.org)

My Next Move (https://www.mynextmove.org)

The emerging techniques and practices relevant to improving cognitive accessibility of information technologies, especially those related to the World Wide Web, are slowly growing momentum as the dire need is recognized for people with intellectual and developmental disabilities (I/DD) to be included in these platforms as a necessity to become culturally and socially integrated into society (Zickuhr & Smith, 2012). The Self-Directed Futures Curriculum (SD.Futures) represents new developments in access through a web-based tool designed to assist with choice making and self-direction in employment exploration and attainment for students with I/DD (Parent-Johnson & Tanis, 2014). Cognitive accessibility features include personalized levels of content accessibility based on an individual student's strengths, error minimization techniques, an innovative choice-making algorithm built into the content to reduce unintended cognitive associations, and multimodal video and audio lesson options. Students work through eight modules focused on identifying their passions, strengths, and career interests; scheduling and participating in their employment team meeting; experiencing and rating community exploration activities; determining their workplace supports; and deciding on adult services resources that are compiled into a final e-portfolio outlining their plan for employment. Prototype development and pilot test results suggest a positive impact on key variables related to student outcomes indicating the potential for future application of the technology.

Consumer Situational Assessment Form

Person Completing Form: _____   Date: _____

Customer: _____

Directions

Indicate the response for each item in the appropriate category based on information gathered from the customer's parent or trainer and from observations made during the situational assessments. For each item, describe the behavior, characteristics, or activity. When applicable, include the frequency of its occurrence and the environment where it occurs (antecedent, consequences, location, and people).

	Parent or Guardian	Other	Situational Assessment I	Situational Assessment II	Situational Assessment III
Strength: Lifting and carrying Poor (<10 lb) Fair (10–20 lb) Average (30–40 lb) Strong (>50 lb)					
Endurance Works <2 hours Works 2–3 hours Works 3–4 hours Works >4 hours					
Orienting Small area only One room Several rooms Building-wide Building and grounds					
Physical mobility Sit/stand in one area Fair ambulation Stairs/minor obstacles Physical abilities					
Independent work rate (No prompts) Slow pace Steady/average pace Above average Sometimes fast Continual fast pace					

Figure 4.2. Consumer situational assessment form. (From: Virginia Commonwealth University/Rehabilitation Research and Training Center [revised 2/94]. Adapted from the VCU-RRTC Consumer Employment Screening Form.)

(continued)

Figure 4.2. *(continued)*

Page 2 of 5

	Parent or Guardian	Other	Situational Assessment I	Situational Assessment II	Situational Assessment III
Appearance Unkempt/poor hygiene Unkempt/clean Neat/clean but clothing unmatched Neat/clean and clothing matched					
Communication Uses sounds/gestures Uses key words/signs Speaks unclearly Communicates clearly, intelligibly to strangers					
Social interactions Rarely interacts appropriately Polite, responses appropriate Initiates social interactions infrequently Initiates social interactions					
Attention to task/perseverance Cannot perform tasks in sequence Performs 2–3 tasks in sequence Performs 4–6 tasks in sequence Performs 7 or more tasks in sequence					
Initiative/motivation Always seeks work Sometimes volunteers Waits for directions Avoids next task					

Figure 4.2. *(continued)*

Page 3 of 5

	Parent or Guardian	Other	Situational Assessment I	Situational Assessment II	Situational Assessment III
Adapting to change Adapts to change Adapts to change with some difficulty Adapts to change with great difficulty Rigid routine					
Reinforcement needs Frequently required Daily Weekly Paycheck sufficient					
Level of support Very supportive of work Supportive of work with reservations Indifferent about work Negative about work					
Discrimination skills Cannot distinguish between work supplies Distinguishes between work supplies with an external cue Distinguishes between work supplies					
Time awareness Unaware of time and clock function Identifies breaks/lunch Can tell time to the hour Can tell time in hours and minutes					

(continued)

Figure 4.2. *(continued)*   Page 4 of 5

	Parent or Guardian	Other	Situational Assessment I	Situational Assessment II	Situational Assessment III
Independent street crossing None 2-lane street (with or w/o light) 4-lane street (with or w/o light)					
Handling criticism/stress Resistive/ argumentative Withdraws into silence Accepts criticism/ does not change					
Acts/speaks aggressively Hourly Daily Weekly Monthly Never					
Travel skills Requires bus training Uses bus independently (with or w/o transfers) Able to make own travel arrangements					
Unusual behavior None Few Many					
Work experience Employment site Job tasks performed Dates, hours, wages					
Physical limitations Impairment Medications Medical restrictions					

Figure 4.2. *(continued)* Page 5 of 5

	Parent or Guardian	Other	Situational Assessment I	Situational Assessment II	Situational Assessment III
Responding to survival words Street signs Restrooms Danger, stop					
Leisure skills/ interests					
Chores or responsibilities					
Activities, foods, and items that are reinforcing					
Money skills Discriminates between coins Makes minor purchases Makes major purchases Amount of spending Money given to customer Willingness of family to give customer money from paycheck					
Asking for assistance Peers Coworkers Acquaintances Persons in authority					
Other					

Situational Assessment Observational Form

Worker's name: _____   Date: _____

Observer's name: _____   Title: _____

Instructions

This form is used to record your observations during situational assessments conducted at multiple businesses in the community. For each setting, write down the tasks performed, characteristics of the work environment, and the job skills demonstrated by the individual. It is important to note that the worker is not expected to be able to perform the job during the short situational assessment period. What is important is identifying the strengths and talents exhibited by the person under specific conditions across multiple settings. For example, consider interactions with coworkers, physical capabilities, fine and gross motor skills, work ethic and behaviors, response to trainers, orienting around the business, asking questions, reactions to corrections, talents and passions, task completion, and any other aspect of the work experience that you observe. Do not interpret the individual's actions or record with your subjective opinion but rather write only your objective observation during the assessment. For example, say "Jason did not perform the task when asked or prompted" rather than "Jason does not like folding towels because he refused to do the job." Be sure to make note of any supports or strategies that helped the individual learn and perform the job.

Observations

Job 1:

Job 2:

Job 3:

Synthesis

What themes did you identify across work assessments?

What are the individual's strengths?

What are the individual's support needs?

What recommendations would you suggest to help this person become competitively employed?

What other ideas or strategies do you recommend?

Figure 4.3.   Situational assessment observational form.

Planning the Transition to Employment by Wendy S. Parent-Johnson, Laura A. Owens, and Richard Parent-Johnson.

PROVIDING COMMUNITY WORK AND INTERNSHIP OPPORTUNITIES

Participating with local businesses in work-based learning opportunities, such as internships and apprenticeships, can provide valuable work experiences for skills development. In addition, students have the opportunity to find out about the kinds of jobs they like and the characteristics of different work environments that are most attractive to them. Perhaps most important, students have the chance to learn the meaning of work, develop a work ethic, and practice how to be a good coworker. A well-known example of an established internship program focused on employment is Project Search (http://www.projectsearch.us).

Originating from a business model developed by Erin Riehle, nursing director with Cincinnati Children's Hospital, Project Search is a 1-year school-to-work program implemented at the workplace and offering classroom instruction, career exploration, and hands-on training all at the business site (Daston, Riehle, & Rutkowski, 2012). In 2019, Project Search has expanded to nearly 600 program sites across the United States, within the federal government, and in multiple countries such as England, Canada, and Australia. The program boasts an impressive success rate of 70.2% for its participants who became gainfully employed in integrated settings working more than 16 hours a week and earning prevailing wages. In 2016–2017, Project Search participants were reported to earn an average of $9.98 per hour and work an average of 26.3 hours per week (https://www.projectsearch.us/).

A similar innovative state-level initiative called Project Skills is a joint venture in South Dakota between the Division of Vocational Rehabilitation and the Department of Education (https://dhs.sd.gov/rehabservices/projectskills.aspx). This program offers transition-age youth paid work experience in a business for 50 to 250 hours per year and can occur annually throughout high school. Students complete real jobs and receive above minimum wage paid for by vocational rehabilitation. The school provides job coach support, acts as liaison to the employer, and assists the student with learning the job and obtaining permanent employment.

Most recent data for FFY 2017 reports 453 students working through Project Skills with 98% of them identified as having a severe disability (SD Division of Rehabilitation Services [SDDRS], 2018). Since 2009, 806 youth have become successfully employed following their participation in Project Skills (SDDRS, 2018). For example, Bryan, a high school student with an emotional behavioral disorder, participated in Project Skills through his school. His assessment information indicated that he was artistic, liked working on the computer, enjoyed small numbers of people, and was very social once he got to know others. He had hopes of advancing his art but did not have aspirations of going to college. The teacher identified an office environment that was actually a smaller department within a larger business. He had a small group of coworkers whom he worked with daily, but he performed his duties at a workstation that gave him the privacy he preferred. Bryan was also matched to the graphics designer in the department, so in addition to completing clerical duties, he was afforded the opportunity to participate in the creative development of products, social media, and marketing communication.

Bryan made such an impression on his employer with the contributions he made that he was hired by the business before his 250 hours were completed, earning $10.00 an hour and working 30 hours a week with the potential to expand once he completed his school year.

Community-based work experiences are an essential component of a student's educational program and can be implemented in a variety of creative ways. One idea is to connect with the

RESEARCH

Paid employment while in school is the greatest indicator of paid employment after finishing school (Simonsen, Fabian, & Luecking, 2015; Wehman, 2011).

established career and technical education (CTE) program at the school and support the participation of students with disabilities in the training and vocational experiences they offer. A second strategy might be to assist students with obtaining summer employment with support from vocational rehabilitation or the school through enrollment in an extended school year. Tapping into other available opportunities, such as apprenticeship programs that may exist at the school or in the community, can provide valuable opportunities for students to gain experience in an area of interest. It is important to note that advocacy may be the first step to enable students with disabilities to be able to participate in these types of programs targeted for the regular student body. In addition, providing support for the student and instructor is critical to ensure a meaningful experience for that individual as well as to open doors for future students to benefit.

RESOURCE

The Office of Special Education and Rehabilitative Services (OSERS) is pleased to publish *A Transition Guide to Postsecondary Education and Employment for Students and Youth with Disabilities*. This guide was issued in 2017 by OSERS, the Rehabilitation Services Administration, and the Office of Special Education Programs to advance efforts in ensuring that all students and youth with disabilities are equipped with the skills and knowledge to be engaged in the 21st-century workforce.

Even without established programs, many teachers make community-based work experiences happen for their students. Developing relationships with the business community and contacting them to inquire about having students in a volunteer or paid capacity can often result in a positive, permanent site location. It is a good idea to develop multiple settings so that students gain a variety of experiences in different types of jobs and different environments in similar types of jobs. For example, many students are identified as liking animals, and often, a goal of working at a humane society is established. One student visited eight different worksites involving animals, such as a dog wash, gourmet dog biscuit shop, pet hotel, nature center, veterinary office, pet supply store, and an animal shelter, and worked for a while in some of them. This resulted in the student not liking the animal shelter but instead choosing a veterinary office. Why? The animal shelter was loud and smelled unpleasant, whereas the clinic was quieter, cleaner, and less hectic. These environmental nuances so critical to an individual's employment and not something they are aware of or can express constitute one of the exceedingly important benefits of being in a variety of real work settings. One rule of thumb is to start early with multiple worksites and gradually become more specific as the student's interests start becoming evident and he or she is getting closer to graduation.

For example, Jason attended a self-contained classroom due to the expectation that he was not ready for employment. During his last year of school, his teacher took him out to a restaurant to see how he would do as a dishwasher. He refused to work and was very disruptive, so she took him out to the lobby area. Jason saw a bus person and expressed an interest in that task. The teacher arranged for him to bus tables, which he enjoyed and did well. Her response: "I never thought Jason would be able to do any job and am very surprised to see just how good a worker he can be." This one eye-opening illustration of Jason's competencies changed his school program and potential postschool employment outcome in ways that no classroom instruction or reporting by others could accomplish.

A common mistake is to provide work experiences but fail to treat them as real jobs, resulting in students doing only a small portion of the position requirements, not being held to the same employee

RESOURCE

Help students learn about the world of work and the rules governing their employment as well as where to go if they have any questions at YouthRules! (https://www.youthrules.dol.gov), a U.S. Department of Labor initiative.

expectations, or being segregated with other students with disabilities and consequently never being challenged to learn or gain the full experience or be included in the work culture. It is important that the same procedures for employment be followed and that the student be held to those expectations but receive the essential training and support to be able to learn how to perform the duties of the job. Even if the student does not like the task, learning how to work through that task and get to more enjoyable tasks is an important work-related skill to be learned. Interacting with others, asking questions, offering assistance, and taking breaks together are critical for learning the soft skills that are so hard to teach in an abstract classroom situation and too often are the cause for someone not staying successfully employed. If a teacher steps in or avoids these critical teaching moments, the student loses the chance to gain practice opportunities for developing these essential work-related skills.

Finally, it is important to collect data on the student's performance at the internship. Having the employer complete an evaluation (Figure 4.4) provides a realistic view of the student's performance and the needs of the business.

ESTABLISHING EMPLOYMENT OR POSTSECONDARY EDUCATION AREAS OF INTEREST

The key to all of the activities described in this chapter is to get to know each and every student in ways that go beyond their disability label and limitations that often follow them. Each student's assets are more enhanced when matched to the right environment and combined with the right supports. Spending time in a variety of environments and settings outside the classroom provides the opportunity to know who this student is, what he or she likes and does not like, what his or her interests and passions are, and what types of supports he or she needs and responds to best. Summarizing this information so it can be shared with adult services agencies and employment support staff is helpful to guide their efforts in finding that best job match. An added advantage of being in community businesses for school personnel is to gain insight into what employers are looking for, which can provide a useful framework for describing an individual's work contributions for use by those who will be helping the student become employed. Another important audience is other school personnel. Think how valuable the information you share can be for your student's next teacher or related school personnel who are involved in his or her education and postschool goals. Often, a progress report highlighting key information and recommendations can be useful. A common complaint among recipients when youth with complex needs are referred is the large file of historical information that follows them and can be difficult and time intensive to sift through to capture the relevant points. One strategy is the use of an e-portfolio that presents the student's important information in a format that is transferable and easily shared by the student himself or herself. It is important to ensure that the summary of information is concise, functional, and contributes to the student's overall postschool goals. This assessment summary of the student becomes his or her present level of performance to guide IEP planning for the upcoming year and/or adult services employment planning and service delivery upon graduation.

Adult Services Provider Vignette

Zane was a young man with mental health and behavioral issues. He was referred to an adult services agency to assist him in finding a job. Mr. Smith began spending time with Zane at school, home, and in the community. Mr. Smith observed that Zane was very interested in drawing and wanted to be a comic book artist. Mr. Smith noticed that Zane was very quiet and enjoyed doing tasks at his own

Employee Progress Report

Company: _____ Date: _____

Employee: _____ Start date: _____

Job duties: _____

_____

Work schedule (days/hours per week): _____

Please rate your employee in the following areas:

	Needs improvement		Good		Excellent
Attendance:	1	2	3	4	5
Understands job duties:	1	2	3	4	5
Completes job duties effectively:	1	2	3	4	5
Productivity:	1	2	3	4	5
Accuracy/quality of work:	1	2	3	4	5
Remains focused on the job:	1	2	3	4	5
Takes initiative/ self-starter:	1	2	3	4	5
Interacts with coworkers/ customers:	1	2	3	4	5
Grooming/hygiene:	1	2	3	4	5
Follows instructions	1	2	3	4	5
Overall performance to date:	1	2	3	4	5

Explanation for ratings of excellent or needs improvement and specific concerns regarding work performance:

What other duties can the employee do to expand his or her role increase value to your business?

Signature of person completing form: _____ Title: _____

Figure 4.4. Employee progress report. (*Source:* Creative Employment Opportunities, Milwaukee, WI, www.ceomke.com).

pace. Zane also preferred late afternoon and evening over early morning visits. When Zane was completing a task, he concentrated on that task to completion. However, when people were around, Zane had difficulty focusing and completing tasks. A Positive Personal Profile (PPP) was developed and used to create an individualized job development plan. While Zane's career goal was to be a comic book artist, Mr. Smith observed and talked with Zane and others to identify what he enjoyed about drawing. Zane liked being able to work at his own pace, work alone, and work on multiple drawings. Mr. Smith talked with a large local law firm and customized a job in the mailroom where Zane worked second shift with only one other coworker, could work at his own pace, and worked on multiple projects. Zane still draws for fun and still has a dream of drawing for a comic book, but he now has a job that he enjoys and that pays the bills.

SUMMARY

School is a time for learning and exploring options for making career and college choices after graduation. Students with disabilities need inclusive classroom and community-based experiences to develop skills and identify their interests and passions to prepare them for post-school employment. Vocational training, job shadowing, work experiences, internships, and situational assessments offer opportunities for accessing real-world experiences in community businesses and gaining the richness of instruction that these settings provide. The added benefit is teacher and student self-assessments of individual skills, interests, work environments, and passions that contribute to curriculum development while in school and employment after graduation. Sharing this information with adult services personnel is important for ensuring a good job match and contributing to successful employment outcomes. Teachers can enhance this process by having high expectations for all students that guide their instruction, planning, and communication regarding vocational preparation and career exploration.

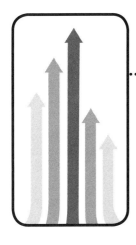

5

Developing Employer Relationships to Create Job Opportunities

Ms. Beckman learned about the importance of networking at a conference she attended. The presenter suggested that teachers connect with people they know or with whom they do business. Ms. Beckman decided to start her networking with the school board members, all of whom were connected to the community and local business in some way. She wrote a letter to her superintendent asking to present at the next school board meeting about the transition services their district offers and how school board members might be able to assist. She presented with a small group of students who talked about their current work experiences and how important work was to them. Ms. Beckman then asked each board member to consider being a part of the transition services. She explained that the students would be graduating and staying in their community, and as school board members, it would say a lot if each board member would commit to assist with mock interviews, review résumés, and/or talk with their employers about providing work experiences or employment for students. As a result, half the board members contacted her to schedule meetings with their employers to establish a collaborative relationship with the district around transition, and several more agreed to come to the school once a quarter to talk with the students about employment-related skills, including conducting mock interviews.

COMPETITIVE INTEGRATED EMPLOYMENT

Competitive integrated employment—employment on the payroll of a local business—is the gold standard for transition-age youth (Allison, Hyatt, Owens, Clark, & Test, 2017). Research has shown that the best predictor of postschool success is paid employment while students are still in school (e.g., Benz, Lindstrom, & Yovanoff, 2000; Carter, Austin, & Trainor, 2012; Test et al., 2009). Legislation such as the Workforce Innovation and Opportunity Act (WIOA) of 2014 (PL 113-128) and Employment First initiatives have increased the focus on competitive integrated employment for youth and adults with disabilities.

Section 404 of the WIOA (2014) defines competitive integrated employment as work that is performed on a full-time or part-time basis for which an individual is 1) compensated at or above minimum wage or commensurate with individuals without disabilities performing similar duties and with similar training and experience, 2) eligible for the level of benefits provided to other employees, 3) at a location where the employee interacts with other individuals without disabilities, and 4) presented opportunities for advancement similar to those of other employees without disabilities in similar positions. In addition to the WIOA, most states now have Employment First initiatives (policies, executive orders, legislation), which emphasize competitive integrated employment as the first and preferred outcome for individuals with disabilities, regardless of the type or severity of disability. It is important for students with disabilities to have the same opportunities for employment as students without disabilities through jobs after school, on weekends, or during the summer.

As you begin to assist students in obtaining competitive integrated employment, it is important to understand the difference between job development and job placement. Job placement, simply put, is getting a job. The process of job placement is relatively simple and what most of us do for ourselves. We identify employers who are hiring, find jobs we are interested in doing, apply, interview, and get hired. Job placement identifies jobs that are already available, "off-the-shelf" jobs, putting the job seeker in direct competition with other job seekers who do not have disabilities that could limit employment opportunities. Job placement is not a bad way of finding employment for a job seeker with a disability, but it is not the only way. Job development focuses on building employer relationships and creating opportunities that may not have existed previously in the business. The job development process matches the interests and needs of the job seeker with the needs of the business. Presenting to your school board is a great way to begin connecting with the business community. School board members are often in business and can make introductions to decision makers who can talk with you about providing work experiences and hiring students with disabilities.

➡ **TIP**   Have students present to the school board about the importance of internships and integrated employment from their personal experience. After the presentation, have students write thank-you notes to the school board members asking whom they know in the business community who would be interested in hearing more about hiring them. Consider asking board members to come to observe students working in the community to see the importance of work-based learning experiences.

KNOWING THE BUSINESS COMMUNITY

As an educator, you are an expert in teaching and supporting individuals with disabilities. However, you may not feel confident in working with the business community. When meeting with employers, strike a balance between preparedness for a conversation with a decision maker and an attitude of active curiosity regarding the unmet needs of the business. Remind employers that many of their employees may have gone to school and had classes with students who had disabilities and will be comfortable working alongside a coworker with a disability. While the primary responsibility of a good job developer is to listen, it is also important to arm ourselves with the knowledge of how and why our students make excellent employees. In order for you to develop business relationships, it is important to have some knowledge of the business as well as of the student.

Businesses have four goals: 1) save money, 2) save time, 3) generate new business, and 4) make a profit. You can help businesses with all four of these goals by knowing your students and the business. Students are potential employees who want to work, and you have the ability to prescreen candidates according to what the employer is looking for (saving time and money). You can also help generate new business by letting people know about employers who hire individuals with disabilities. Hiring a student with a disability might help create an environment that encourages people with disabilities to patronize that business.

CASE STUDY   A local retail store hired an individual who uses a wheelchair. The new employee noted that the aisles were difficult to maneuver in a wheelchair because items were so close together and preferred items were located on upper shelves. The store manager made note of these suggestions and, during inventory week, reorganized the layout of the store. Ultimately, this led to an increase in the number of customers with physical disabilities shopping at this store.

In general, employers look for three characteristics in employees they hire—with or without disabilities: 1) reliability/dependability, 2) availability/flexability, and 3) productivity/quality of work. Employers are looking for employees who are reliable and dependable, come to work on time, complete their job duties/tasks, and take the initiative when they see tasks that need to be done. Employers also are looking at employees who are available and flexible to work when the employer needs them to work. For example, a business may be looking for employees willing to work weekends, holidays, before 9 a.m. or after 5 p.m., or they may need people who are on call depending on the type of business. Finally, employers are looking for employees who are productive and/or provide quality work—employees who get the job done in a timely fashion and to the specifications required. One important caveat is that employers are often willing to negotiate on any of these areas depending on their needs. For example, a retailer during the holiday season might need employees who come to work every day and are flexible with their schedule, but the retailer may be willing to negotiate on the productivity or quality of work during that time. Taking time to understand the needs of the business is essential.

CASE STUDY   Mr. Lopez, the central supply manager at a local hospital, was always hiring new employees to work the 6 a.m. to 2 p.m. shift. In addition, he noted that many people used the entry-level positions to move to other positions throughout the hospital. Porter, the employment consultant, discussed his needs during the informational interview, and Mr. Lopez explained that he needed an employee who was reliable and flexible in his or her schedule—who could, for example, stay longer on high surgery days or work weekends. He also explained that quality and productivity was also important. After touring the area and further discussions, Porter and Mr. Lopez identified the critical need as reliability and flexibility. While quality and productivity were important, they were able to negotiate a workaround in which the student would initially work on days that were not high surgery days so she could learn the job. When asked how quality was monitored with other employees, Mr. Lopez said there was no consistent method. Porter suggested that the new employee be partnered with a mentor veteran. The new employee could assemble the surgical trays for the day, and the mentor employee could wrap the trays for sterilization and quality check while wrapping. After 3 months, Mr. Lopez noted that the partner system had increased productivity and quality, and most important, he implemented the surgical tray assembly partner system with other employees to ensure quality throughout the department.

BUSINESS KNOWLEDGE

Understanding that employers want people who stay with the company—saving them time and money in recruitment and training—is important. Researching what employers are looking for—what their industry looks like now and in the future—is a big part of job development. Each business looks for a different mix of skills and experience depending on the industry. Even with national chains, business needs may differ depending on the location. For example, a Target store in Milwaukee, Wisconsin, may have very different needs than a Target in Gulfport, Mississippi. Knowing all aspects of a business guides job development in identifying what tasks need to be done and what may not be getting done. It is important to remember that an employer will hire anyone as long as they believe that the new employee will increase profit and lower costs to their business.

In order to meet the needs of businesses, it is important to develop an understanding of industry expectations for the future, workplace culture, job conditions, turnover rate, and bottom-line concerns of employers. Educators must find ways to reach outside of the school community and interact with local businesses through networking and presenting to business groups (Box 5.1).

Box 5.1.   Before You Start: Food for Thought

Business Knowledge

1. Can you identify common needs in this type of business?
2. Can you speak the "language" of the business?
3. Do you know the business buzz words?
4. Can you identify educational/adult services terms that might be unfamiliar to an employer?
5. Can you identify educational/human services terms that might detract from your presentation?

Business Approach

1. Do you have professional materials (e.g., business cards, brochure, video, presentation book)?
2. Is your presentation clear, complete, and organized?
3. Are your objectives clearly defined?
4. Have you had your presentation critiqued by an employer?

Prospecting

1. Have you identified (in your mind) all of the things you would like to have in a job?
2. Have you identified the points you will not compromise on?
3. Do you have a good system to store the information gathered?
4. Are you pursuing enough leads to get the desired results?
5. After successful placements, are you getting referrals? Are you asking?
6. Do you have a sample script/letter for introductory and follow-up calls?
7. When phoning, are you free of distractions?
8. Do you make several calls in one sitting?
9. Are you prepared for common objections?
10. Do you follow up to confirm the appointment?

Presentations

1. Do you think of yourself as a businessperson?
2. Have you done research on the company?
3. Do you have business cards?
4. Do you have clear, organized, and updated materials?
5. Do you know exactly how long your presentation will take?
6. Do you know what information you need to get from the employer?
7. Do you have an idea of key questions to ask?
8. Do you have a goal or established need to be met?
9. Can you demonstrate your ability to meet that goal/need?
10. Are you familiar with different closing statements?
11. Do you have materials to leave behind?
12. Have you critiqued your last presentation and made appropriate changes?

Remember: You will get 10 no answers for every 1 yes answer!

Source: Creative Employment Opportunities, Milwaukee, WI, www.ceomke.com

NETWORKING

What? Talking to complete strangers? Yes, that is what you need to do! Networking is the most important way of connecting with the business community. Job development can best be described as identifying, recruiting, and maintaining relationships with businesses and other organizations that will result in competitive integrated employment opportunities for students. Talk to employers who have already hired students with disabilities or who have provided job shadows or work-based learning experiences, and ask for referrals to other businesses. Ask the employer to provide an introduction to one new employer he or she knows. A great starting point is with those businesses where a relationship has been established through previous work arrangements (e.g., job shadows, workplace tours, work-based learning) or those places frequented as a customer.

Another group of employers are businesses where you or the job seeker currently do business. Everyone is currently a customer of some other business. Everyone has a personal sphere of influence: Immediate family and distant relatives; close friends and casual acquaintances; people you do business with, such as your mail carrier, plumber, tailor, barber, dry cleaner, deli counter clerk, and gas station attendant; and people who do business with you–family members, other businesses, school personnel, and school board members. The networking form shown in Figure 5.1 is an example that can be used to keep track of contacts of your students, family members and even your own.

There are two types of job leads: Those found through the open market and those found in the hidden market. Job placement focuses on open market jobs, those brought to the public's attention through advertising and want ads. Jobs found on the open market often do not address the specific skills of individuals with disabilities. Jobs in the hidden market, on the other hand, do not rely on competition but on personal connections; approximately 80% of jobs are found through the hidden market and they are often better jobs.

There are many business groups, such as the local chamber of commerce, Rotary clubs, Lions clubs, small business associations, and others. Most business groups have events, such as business after-hours or networking lunches, and attending these events gives you opportunities to engage with the business community. If your school district is not a member of the local chamber of commerce, find out how to become a member. Often, administrators (e.g., superintendents) are the key contacts of local chambers of commerce. As an educator, find out from your administration who attends chamber meetings and provide that person with information about hiring students with disabilities. Offer to attend a meeting with your district person in addition to participating in chamber activities and events. Attending chamber or business events is one way to tap into the hidden job market, identify new business ideas and leads, and support new projects.

If there are no events to attend in your community, create your own. Arrange face-to-face meetings with people you know and businesses in your community to get to know them better. As an educator, networking opportunities occur constantly–anywhere, anytime. Wherever you go, whether out to eat, grocery shopping, to get your hair cut, or to pick up dry cleaning, you are always connecting with people who might be helpful in connecting you with other businesses. Offer to make a presentation to groups and business organizations, and bring students and businesspeople with whom you are working to present with you.

➡ **TIP**   When talking with employers, it is important to use terminology that will open further discussion. Using terms such as *creating* or *carving* jobs may end the discussion, as employers typically do not see creating or carving jobs for individuals as beneficial to their business. Under the Americans with Disabilities Act (ADA) of 1990 (PL 101-336), the term *job restructuring* is considered a possible reasonable accommodation. Under the ADA, job restructuring includes modifications such as reallocating or redistributing marginal job functions that an employee is unable to perform because of a disability or altering when and/or how a function, essential or marginal, is performed. It is important to note the ADA is clear that an employer is not required to reallocate essential functions as a reasonable accommodation but can do so if they want. When developing jobs, focus on the needs of the business as well as the potential employee and use terms such as *job restructuring*. Interview the employer about the business and job tasks that need to get done that may not be getting done to begin the conversation of restructuring jobs.

Networking

Write down the name of *anyone* who comes to mind. Do not worry about whether that person will remember you or whether he or she will know of any job openings at this time.

Friends

_____

_____

Neighbors

_____

_____

People from religious organizations

_____

_____

People who provide service to me (child care provider, grocer, bank teller, dry cleaner)

_____

_____

Relatives

_____

_____

People from social/athletic organizations

_____

_____

Former classmates/instructors

_____

_____

Relatives of significant other

_____

_____

Former employers/coworkers

_____

_____

Friends of parents/relatives

_____

_____

Other

_____

_____

Figure 5.1. Networking form. (From Creative Employment Opportunities, Milwaukee, Wisconsin. Adapted with permission.)

Figure 5.1. *(continued)* Page 2 of 2

MY NETWORK

Name	Contact Number	How can they help?

MEETING WITH EMPLOYERS

The purpose of the initial meeting should be to find out as much as possible about the business. The primary goal for you is to have the employer articulate the business's needs. Sometimes employers will start by asking about what you do, so it is important to respond, "I'd love to tell you about what we do, but first I need to know more about you–so what I'd like to do is ask you some questions," and design your questions to facilitate a conversation about the business. "Are you hiring people in entry-level positions?" is not a good question because it does not give you enough information. Take control by designing your questions to obtain the information you need to create opportunities for your students–interview the employer.

Conducting an informational interview is a great way to start your employer relationship. The purpose of the informational interview is to obtain information and advice about a particular business or industry. It is your way of getting to know more about the needs of a business–just as you got to know about the interests of your student. Job development is about asking questions and listening–listening draws out acceptance instead of resistance on behalf of the employer. When conducting your informational interview, if possible, interview employees as well. Often, they will have some key information about tasks that need to get done that they may not be able to get to. For example, when conducting an informational interview combined with a tour of a small local insurance company in a rural community, the interviewer asked two employees about the work they did. The conversation resulted in a discussion about the amount of copying and number of mailings they needed to do on a weekly basis, which took them away from their primary responsibilities. This information was essential to developing the employment proposal to present to the employer, which included copying and mailings as part of the duties for the customized position developed.

Learning how to conduct an informational interview–how to question–is important. You do not want to simply rattle off question after question, or it will sound like the Spanish Inquisition! When asking questions, it is important to phrase them in a way that will give you as much information as possible–using open rather than closed questions. A closed question can be answered with a single word or a short phrase. For example, "How old are you?" and "Where do you live?" are closed questions. A closed question can often be answered with either yes or no and does not give you much information. An open question is more likely to engage the employer in a conversation about the business. Open questions can also contain the information you are looking for, subtly prompting the employer to answer in a particular way–for example, "How much turnover will you have in the next 3–6 months?" or "What skills and abilities do you look for to do this job?" Asking an employer what is not getting done that needs to get done is a key question (see informational interview questions in Figure 5.2).

Your initial conversation should always be about the needs of the employer–the informational interview is designed to draw out employer needs (we ask job seekers what they need and

WAYS TO CLOSE A MEETING

- Order pad: I have three candidates right now who are interested in working in this field. I'd like to bring them in for a (e.g., tour, job shadow, internship).
- Choice question: Since you have a great deal to offer our students, I wonder if you would have time to (serve on our business advisory board, assist us in conducting mock interviews once a month, provide a tour to our students, schedule a meeting with department heads, etc.).
- Impending event: In August, discuss with employers their needs now that the college students will be going back to school and if they may have positions to fill, or ask about hiring for the holiday season (Employers typically begin filling holiday positions in August.).

Informational Interview

Company name: _____   Date: _____

Employer name/position: _____

Questions to Ask Employer	Responses
In your opinion, what are some unique qualities your company possesses (what seems to distinguish your company from its competitors)? What is your company's mission? What do you value?	
What are some current trends in the field? Where will the growth be? What will change? How do you think the skills needed today might change compared with skills needed tomorrow?	
Can you give me a general idea of the range of jobs that exist here (or within the organization)?	
What about secondary job duties for staff (e.g., those little tasks that are neglected because people do not always have time to complete them)?	
How do you recruit employees? What attributes/basic skills are needed to be successful in this company/field?	
What is the typical hiring process?	
Do you have any recurring human resource challenges?	
Do you have any additional unmet needs or log jams in the organization?	

General Observations
(These are not questions to ask but observations to make.)

1. What is the company site culture, and how would you describe the environment (the feel of the place)?

2. Are there miscellaneous tasks that might be compiled into a new position?

3. If this company has other site operations (warehouse, distributing center, etc.) within the area, would it be willing to help set up a site visit there?

Figure 5.2. Informational interview. (From: TransCen, Inc., Rockville, MD, www.transcen.org; reprinted with permission.)   *(continued)*

Figure 5.2. *(continued)* Page 2 of 2

Informational Interview Questions

Overview
1. Describe your products and/or services.
2. In your opinion, what are some unique qualities your company possesses?
3. What distinguishes your company from its competitors?
4. What are the trends in the field?
5. Where will the growth be?
6. What are the skills needed today versus in the future?

Workforce
7. How many employees do you currently have?
8. Can you give me a general idea of the range of jobs that exist within your organization?
9. Which jobs have the highest number of employees?
10. Which jobs are full time, and which jobs are part time?
11. Which jobs turn over the most?
12. What are some of the reasons these jobs turnover?
13. Which jobs are hardest to fill, and why?
14. What job openings do you have at this time?
15. What have been your experiences hiring special types of employees such as seniors, students, or youth just out of school?
16. What has been your experience in working with employment agencies in the past?

Jobs That Potentially Match Your Caseload
17. What are the tasks required to do this job?
18. What skills and abilities do you look for to do this job?
19. Are there any minimum requirements that job candidates must have to be considered for this job?
20. What type of personality is best suited to do this type of work?
21. What are the pay range and benefits related to this job?
22. Do you have a probationary period for this type of job?
23. How are new employees trained for this type of job?

Recruitment
24. How do you recruit your employees?
25. Do you have a sense of how much it costs your company in time and money to recruit, hire, and train new employees?
26. Do you work with any other community programs (such as the local career center) to recruit new employees? If so, what has been your experience with those programs?

Hiring Process
27. What is the typical hiring process?
28. Specifically, what are you looking for on the application and/or résumé and cover letter?
29. Do job candidates have to apply online, or are there other options?
30. If job candidates have to apply online, do they also have to take any tests or surveys? If so, what are you looking for on those tests/surveys?
31. What is the interviewing process? What are some of the key questions that are asked during the interviews?
32. How would you characterize a successful interview based on what you are looking for in the job candidate?
33. Would it be helpful to you if we let you know when one of our prescreened candidates has applied online?
34. Who makes the final hiring decision?

Workforce-Related Issues (Productivity)
35. Do you have any recurring human resource challenges?
36. Do you have peak times of day, week, or season related to your operations? If so, how do you address those peak demands for labor?
37. Do you use temporary employment services? If so, how often and for what types of tasks?
38. Do you have to pay overtime? If so, how often, and which types of jobs are paid for overtime?
39. Do you have any additional unmet labor needs or log jams in the organization?
40. Are there secondary job duties that key employees in your organization do not always have time to get to? If so, what are the tasks that these key employees have trouble completing in a timely manner?

Wrap Up
41. Would it be possible to observe specific types of jobs being done or specific areas of the company?
42. Could we schedule another 20- to 25-minute appointment? I want to put some information together and go over how our employment services could benefit your company.

want–we must ask employers the same). Always close the meeting with a way to maintain the relationship, whether to come back for a tour or to talk with a specific manager. Your closing question should be "When is our next meeting?"

EMPLOYMENT PROPOSALS

Developing an employment proposal is a way to create or restructure positions to meet the needs of the business and job seeker. Creating opportunities based on the needs of the business and talents of the job seeker is what job development is all about (Figure 5.3). Employment proposals are developed to negotiate a job description in which tasks from other job descriptions are identified and selected to create a new job description on the basis of the unmet needs of the business and the assets and strengths of the job seeker. It is important to provide a clear, written proposal that highlights the cost effectiveness of restructuring positions. Employment proposals focus on the needs of the business and the competencies of the job seeker–they are asset based rather than deficit based. Rather than focusing on what the job seeker is unable to do, the employment proposal focuses on what skills and talents the person will bring to the business.

Overcoming Objections

Objections are often disguised requests for additional information. Take every no as a *not yet,* and listen, listen, listen. Acknowledge the legitimacy of the objection, repeat the objection, and ask questions to pinpoint the specific concern. See Table 5.1 for some sample objections and possible responses.

Following Up and Maintaining Contacts

As you are developing employer relationships, it is important to maintain contact with employers. During the beginning, you may want to touch base once a month to see how things are going in the business or stop by to see how the business is going. Often, going back to the business to observe is a great way to identify opportunities for your students. Be sure to collect and use business cards of all employers you meet, and give them your card. It is very easy to make your own business cards; be sure they are focused on business rather than social services. Create signature touchpoints, such as holidays and birthdays, and refer other people to the business. After meetings be sure to send personalized, follow-up thank-you notes (not e-mail thank-you notes but handwritten thank-you notes). Develop a database to follow up with your contacts (e.g., use a tickler file or computer database such as ACT!, Filemaker Pro, or Access).

PREPARING STUDENTS FOR EMPLOYMENT THROUGH WORK-BASED LEARNING OR INTERNSHIPS

Work-based learning experiences or internships are opportunities to learn about what job seekers want to do and what they do not want to do. Often, when people start working at their "ideal" job, they realize it is not so ideal for them after all. Most of us tried many different jobs from the time we were in high school through college in order to identify our true career passions. It is important to remember that not all internships work out–but that does not mean they are not successful. We learn from all our experiences, the good, the bad, and even the ugly. Internships are important for all job seekers–including individuals with disabilities. Because the term *internship* is universal, employers understand the concept and often look

Employment Proposal

Employment Proposal for a part-time office assistant at Relief and Wellness Chiropractic Office

Submitted to:	Relief and Wellness Chiropractic Office
Submitted by:	LO, CEO, Inc.
Purpose:	Increase profits by improving rate of customers who keep their appointments by having a staff member who will

    1. Organize customer files.

    2. Contact customers prior to scheduled appointment.

    3. Keep customers informed of special products or events.

    4. Serve as customer advocate by obtaining feedback about ways to expand service.

Candidate:	Elsie C., an independent self-starter who recently completed an office skills class at Independence First. She offers organizational abilities, excellent communication skills, and a cooperative attitude.
How:	Elsie needs access to a computer and phone. She can work 20 hours a week, afternoons or evenings depending on the business needs.
Terms:	Elsie will provide these services for $8/hour, and after the first 3 months if profits increase, she will be given a raise to $11/hour. Elsie will have a support person on the job, through CEO, who will provide modifications and assist her in learning the job.

Employment Proposal for a part-time bakery assistant at Fresh Thyme Farmer's Market

To: WS, Manager Date: April 26, 2018
Proposed Employee: MN
Represented by: JL, Employment Consultant

Rationale
- Increase productivity in bakery by preparing ingredients for recipes, etc.
- Assist with bakery shelving, baking, sorting, stickers
- Increase diversity in the workforce along with understanding of team working with coworkers with diverse needs
- Provide customer service to customers through sharing a positive attitude

Benefit
As a neighborhood store, your mission to improve the way the community eats by offering fresh and healthy food at amazing values in a vibrant and fun shopping environment, with smiling, welcoming faces is enhanced through friendly and diverse employees representing the population of the neighborhoods. Hiring employees with a strong passion to work and share their talents with local customers enhances your mission.

    This proposal describes what a part-time bakery assistant could do for Fresh Thyme Farmers Market to help support employees in the bakery area in order to increase productivity by assisting with tasks needed to complete their jobs.

Job Functions
- Measure ingredients
- Stock supplies from inventory
- Assist with preparing bakery items
- Respond to customer inquiries
- Sticker products to be sold
- Package products
- Date inventory/rotate products

Proposed Employee
- MN is an eager, determined, and enthusiastic individual interested in obtaining work in a bakery. MN has a passion for baking and cooking and is always ready and willing to lend a hand where needed.

Figure 5.3. Sample employment proposals.

Table 5.1. Sample objections and possible responses

"I'm really busy right now."	"I know how busy you must be; your business is really growing. If you could find 15 minutes in the next week, I would like to have the opportunity to talk about your business and find ways to free up your time and possibly save your company money."
"I just don't know if someone with a disability could do the jobs we have."	"I think every employer has that feeling at first. I'm glad you were comfortable enough to let me know. Is your concern over job performance or social behavior? Both? Perhaps we can use the approach we used at ABC company. Why don't we start Antoine on an 8-week trial basis to evaluate whether he meets your expectations? If not, we'll either back off or suggest someone new—your choice. Would that be fair?"
"I'll see if my managers are interested and get back to you."	"Getting your managers involved is a great idea. Do you think any of them have had any experience in working with individuals with disabilities? Our experience at XYZ company was that the managers showed more interest once they had a better idea of our capabilities. Perhaps we could schedule a short presentation to the managers to make sure they know how we might be able to work together. I could even bring in a couple of students to talk about their interests."
"We don't have any openings."	"That's terrific. I'm not here to ask you to hire at this time. I want to learn about your needs so we can respond quickly when you do have an opening. If we could meet for 20 minutes next Tuesday or Wednesday, I'd like to just sit down to hear more about your business."
"I really need employees who are going to work out. I can't take a risk on someone with a disability."	"Do all your employees work out? What are some of the causes when an employee doesn't work out?"

for internships on résumés. They provide opportunities for job seekers to test drive a job to see if they enjoy the ride. In addition, internships allow an employer to "try on" a potential employee. If an internship does not work out, discuss why so that a new plan can be developed. Remember, exposure leads to interests and interests lead to motivation!

➡ **TIP**   Many soft skills can be taught in school and at home. The soft skills that are most important to employers include 1) work ethic, 2) positive attitude, 3) good communication skills, 4) time management, 5) problem solving, 6) teamwork, 7) self-confidence, 8) ability to accept constructive feedback, 9) flexibility, and 10) dealing with stressful situations. During classroom instruction and activities, students should be learning about dedication to a job well done, accepting feedback from teachers, managing their time to complete assignments, communicating their needs (e.g., requesting accommodations in their classes), being resourceful when situations arise, and working with their peers.

Most employers are looking for employees who have good soft job skills (which is why behavioral interviewing and testing is so prevalent today). Soft skills are a cluster of personal qualities, habits, attitudes, and social standards that make someone a good employee and compatible with work in a specific business. Employers value soft skills because research suggests and experience shows that they can be just as important an indicator of job performance as actual job knowledge. In fact, many times an employer would rather hire someone on the basis of soft skills rather than experience or skills on a certain type of job. Employers can teach the hard skills, but they generally lack the time and expertise to teach soft job skills, and there is no better way for job seekers to learn these skills than to jump into a real work environment.

➡ **TIP**   An important addition to internships is to obtain a letter of recommendation from the employer at the end of the internship along with photos or short video clips to include in the job seeker's employment portfolio visual résumé.

PARTNERSHIP AGREEMENT

This agreement can be individualized according to the arrangement with the business and intern. At a minimum, the partnership agreement should include roles and responsibilities of both the business partner and agency. The agreement provided in Figure 5.4 is an example that can be used for future partnerships. Having an agreement shows that this is a professional arrangement and that all parties understand their responsibilities in the process.

➡ **TIP**   Include the district's or agency's certificate of liability insurance with the specific business listed as certificate holder.

WORKSITE ANALYSIS

In tandem with the informational interview, a business site assessment can be conducted. With each business, the different sections may include more or less information depending on the needs of potential interns, environment, job analysis, and staffing. Analyzing the workplace by touring, talking with other employees, and identifying who does what tasks, when, and under what conditions can help in creating integrated employment opportunities (Figure 5.5).

➡ **TIP**   Be sure to include workplace culture information.

INTERN CRITERIA AND JOB DESCRIPTION

As with any job, a job description should be developed for the work experience or internship. The job description could be the standard description the business uses for current employees in that position, or it could be a customized job description you develop through an employment proposal for the internship position.

➡ **TIP**   When customizing a job description, be sure to look at the current and future needs of the business and match them with the interests of the potential intern.

APPLICATION AND INTERVIEW PROCESS

Students should apply for the work experiences or internships they are interested in so they can practice interview skills. The application process should be individualized for the business and intern. Depending on the business agreement, the application used by the business can be utilized, or you may need to create an application specific to the internship. The interview process should also be individualized on the basis of the business agreement and intern. Keep in mind the job seekers with whom you are working to ensure that their interests and talents are highlighted. The purpose of the interview is to focus on the assets of the individual and the value he or she will bring to the business.

➡ **TIP**   Bringing the potential intern to the business for a job shadow is a good idea to include as part of the interview. A hands-on interview, photos, or video clips of the potential intern are also good tools to use.

Internship Business Partner Agreement

[Agency Name] is excited to partner with [Business Name] in providing our prescreened candidates the opportunity to expand their skill sets while serving the needs of your business. As an Internship Business Partner, your business is promoting workplace diversity and equity by providing a series of community work-based training experiences for our job seekers. In order to ensure that our partnership with you is successful, we will provide the following services:

1. [Agency Name] will conduct an Internship Site Assessment.
2. [Agency Name] staff will provide on-the-job and ongoing support for both your business and our candidate during the duration of an internship.
3. [Agency Name] will assist your business in developing a series of internship opportunities.
4. [Agency Name] will assist interns in following the interview and orientation guidelines as determined with [Business Name].

As an Internship Business Partner, you agree to

1. Provide [Agency Name] a business liaison, who will serve as our primary point of contact in coordinating the internships.
2. Provide opportunities for [Agency Name] staff to complete an Internship Site Assessment.
3. Interview prospective internship candidates.
4. Work with [Agency Name] staff on continued development of internship opportunities.
5. Complete an Internship Evaluation at the midpoint and completion of internship experiences. This feedback will allow [Agency Name] staff to continually assess our partnership in order to foster continued success for your business and for future interns.
6. Assist intern with completing and submitting time sheet to [Agency Name] at end of each pay period.

Miscellaneous Internship Program agreements

1. Internships will not exceed a total of 45 days or a total of 40 hours unless agreed upon by all parties.
2. Wages will be paid by [Agency Name], who will also be responsible for liability insurance.
3. This agreement does not require that the intern be hired or imply in any way that the intern will obtain permanent employment through [Business Name].
4. An internship may be terminated by any participating parties at any point.
5. The intern works through [Agency Name] and is not an employee of [Business Name].

_____

Company Representative Signature and Title   Date

_____

School/Agency Representative Signature and Title   Date

Figure 5.4.   Internship business partner agreement. (*Source:* Creative Employment Opportunities, Milwaukee, WI, www.ceomke.com)

Worksite Analysis

Company Name: _____   Contact Person: _____

Address: _____   Phone: _____

Other Key People: _____

Duties/Activities	Currently Performed by	Productivity Requirements	Quality Requirements

Physical Layout/Accessibility	Environmental Conditions (e.g., Noise, Lighting, Temperature)
Social Climate/Work Culture	Special Procedures/Requirements (e.g., Uniform, Check-In Procedures, Quality Standards)
Potential Natural Supports	Health and Safety Factors
Opportunities for Interaction With Others	Opportunities to Expand Into Other Areas/Duties or to Learn Other Skills
Overall Comments	

Figure 5.5. Worksite analysis.

ORIENTATION AND TRAINING

Depending on the business agreement, think about the following questions: 1) Will the intern go through the orientation that hired employees go through, or will there be an individualized orientation for the intern? (This determination might depend on the assets and barriers of the specific intern.) 2) Will there be an agreed-upon amount of time for training that is or is not included in the length of the internship? 3) Who will do the training? Ideally, the business should conduct as much of the orientation and training as possible with the agency/school staff on the side providing support as needed.

EVALUATION PROCESS

Internships should replicate, as close as possible, an actual job throughout the application, interview, and evaluations processes. In order for this to happen, it is important for students to have a variety of experiences based on their passions and interests. PCP is critical as it allows the student to be in the drivers seat and engages everyone in the student's life in the process from family members to neighbors to friends. The evaluation process is designed to help determine the intern's strengths, interests, and areas of support needed and to determine if the job, work tasks, and work environment are a good match for the intern. For example, is the intern making progress in learning? Does he or she enjoy the tasks? Is the work environment suitable for the intern? Employers should be part of the evaluation process that is done, ideally, at the halfway point and again at the end of the internship or work experience; see Figure 5.6. At the end of the internship, a final internship evaluation report should be completed by school or agency staff to summarize all the evaluations and guide plans for future job development (Figure 5.7).

➡ **TIP** Support does not only apply to the intern but also to coworkers and supervisors. This is a great time to provide education and training to the business staff as well and to begin to identify potential "natural" supports on the job.

Box 5.2. A Step-by-Step Approach to Job Development

Business to Business

I. Focus

  A. Target a business

  B. Research the business

    1. Facts and figures

    2. Who is in charge (who is the decision maker)?

    3. Predict the need

  C. Build a strategy

    1. Identify benefits

    2. Use credibility statements/employer references

    3. Provide employer testimonials

    4. Provide supporting literature

  D. Initial contact

    1. Determine "your style" of job development

    2. Request a 15-minute appointment

    3. Start a data card

II. Employer meeting

  A. Consider factors affecting employer receptivity

  B. Set an agenda

(continued)

Box 5.2.   *(continued)*

    C. Present features and benefits as they relate to your service

        1. Incorporate visuals (photos, flow charts, testimonials)

    D. Listen, listen, listen!

        1. Ask questions relevant to the business

        2. Gather information to establish need

    E. Answer objections

    F. Determine next step(s)—leave the door open

        1. Interview (for job or participate in mock interviews)

        2. Tour of company

        3. Feasibility study of potential areas

        4. Additional presentation(s)

        5. Additional information

        6. Phone call follow-up

        7. Other

III. Follow up!

    A. Clarify every step

    B. Implement customer service

IV. Employer recognition

    A. Awards

    B. Publicity

    C. Finishing touches

V. Follow-up is *forever*!

Source: Creative Employment Opportunities, Milwaukee, Wisconsin.

SUMMARY

The purpose of education is to ensure students leave with the skills to be contributing members of their communities. Job development (Box 5.2) is something that everyone–from teachers to students to the superintendent–should be part of. Everyone has connections, including the students and their families. Using a networking sheet (see Figure 5.1) helps students and families understand that they are a part of this process and is helpful in showing with whom they may be connected in the community. The connections from one student and his or her family may benefit other students as well. School is a time to try on different job goals without the "reality police" or idea of job readiness.

It is important to remember that there is no job readiness–we all learn work skills on the job. All employees have a probationary period, during which they demonstrate their value to the business. The question to ask employers is what they expect to see from new employees during the probationary period. Once this is known, the support provided to the employee with a disability focuses on those goals. If employers see progress, if they see the individual providing value to their business, then they will more than likely keep the individual on the job.

Keep in mind that all employees are "supported" employees, and many have "customized" jobs. We all need guidance from family, friends, and coworkers to provide us support on and off the job. Most of us have job descriptions, but many of us do not do all the tasks on our job description equally well. As a result, employers note the strengths that each of us brings to their business, and they customize our job tasks on the basis of what they see we bring to their business. The bottom line is that even for individuals with the most significant disabilities, ways can be found to restructure positions so that they provide value to the business.

Internship Performance Evaluation

Participant Name: _____   Worksite: _____

Date: _____   20-hour review   40-hour review

Performance Rating: 4 = Always 3 = Most of the time   2 = Some of the time   1 = Never

---

1. Dependability

a. Attendance is consistent   4   3   2   1   N/A
b. Arrives to work on time   4   3   2   1   N/A
c. Returns from lunch or break on time   4   3   2   1   N/A
d. Notifies supervisor of illness/absence   4   3   2   1   N/A

2. Personal Appearance

a. General appearance is neat and clean   4   3   2   1   N/A
b. Seems to care about appearance   4   3   2   1   N/A
c. Dress is acceptable for type of work   4   3   2   1   N/A

3. Relationship With Supervisor

a. Listens to instructions   4   3   2   1   N/A
b. Follows through on instructions/training   4   3   2   1   N/A
c. Accepts constructive criticism   4   3   2   1   N/A
d. Requires more than the usual amount of supervision than other new employees   4   3   2   1   N/A

4. Quality of Work

a. Is able to perform all tasks on job description   4   3   2   1   N/A
b. Asks questions when s/he does not understand   4   3   2   1   N/A

5. Quantity of Work

a. After adequate training, works at speed comparable to other employees   4   3   2   1   N/A
b. Is able to work at an acceptable pace throughout work shift   4   3   2   1   N/A

6. Initiative

a. Keeps busy between assignments or when not directly supervised   4   3   2   1   N/A
b. Asks for additional work when completed with assigned tasks   4   3   2   1   N/A

7. Customer Service

a. Friendly and courteous to customers   4   3   2   1   N/A
b. Friendly and courteous to coworkers   4   3   2   1   N/A

8. Overall, how would you rate this participant's performance?

      Excellent   Good   Fair   Needs Improvement

9. Based on this rating, what areas of the participant's performance could be improved upon?

10. Based on this rating, what are the strengths of this participant?

11. Additional Comments:

_____

Supervisor Signature   Date

_____

Supervisor Signature   Date

_____

Staff Signature   Date

Outcome

Continue Internship: YES   NO
Letter of Recommendation: YES   NO
Other:

Figure 5.6.   Internship performance evaluation. (*Source:* Creative Employment Opportunities, Milwaukee, WI).

Final Internship Evaluation

Intern Name: <u>Bryce Johnson</u>
Address: <u>123 Spring Street Summerville, WI 55555</u>
Phone: <u>(414) 555-1212</u>   SS#: <u>333-11-5555</u>
Date of Birth: <u>August 15, 1998</u>
Parent/Guardian: <u>George and Anne Johnson</u>   Phone/e-mail: <u>scj@google.com</u>
Counselor: <u>Porter Smith</u>   Phone/e-mail: <u>414-555-4321/geo@google.com</u>

Host Company: <u>Walgreens</u>
Department(s): <u>General stocking and photo</u>
Supervisor(s): <u>Jeanette Stevens (Patti London, coworker)</u>
Start Date: <u>03/01/18</u>   End Date: <u>04/15/18</u>
Internship Days/Hours

Sunday	Monday	Tuesday	Wednesday	Thursday	Friday	Saturday
	1–4 p.m.	1–4 p.m.	1–4 p.m.	1–4 p.m.	1—4 p.m.	1–4 p.m.

Job duties (list/describe)
Face items on shelves, stock new items that arrive (putting new items forward), assist in photo lab (processing photos), provide customer service

Employment History (past internships, employment, volunteer experiences)
Penzey Spices: Warehouse, 11/1/17 to 12/15/17
Joy Cleaners: Sorting laundry and recycling hangers, 1/15/18 to 2/15/18
Volunteers at the local food pantry every Saturday (has done this for 3 years)

Interests/Preferences
Enjoys being around people but working on his own
Prefers activities that require movement (e.g., both standing and sitting)
Hobbies include riding his bike, Special Olympics (bowling and track), and listening to music (country)

Current Financial Status (Describe benefits that may be affected by employment)
Bryce currently receives SSI; a benefits analysis will be completed to identify the impact his earnings will have on his benefits and possible work incentives that can be used to support him on a job longer term.

Transportation
Bryce currently rides his bike to most activities. He did take the bus to Penzey Spices but is not able to transfer (so a direct bus route would be okay).

Health Status (medication, sensory, communication, personal care needs)
Bryce wears glasses but does not like to wear them and needs to be reminded. He also needs to be reminded to clean his glasses from time to time. Bryce communicates verbally in two- to three-word phrases/sentences. When he is under stress, it can be difficult to understand Bryce. If asked to "say it differently," Bryce will rephrase his question or comment. Bryce takes Ritalin to help him focus.

Figure 5.7. Final internship evaluation.

Figure 5.7. *(continued)* Page 2 of 3

Internship Overview

Evaluate and comment on each work competency listed.
Combine with supervisor's evaluation to develop recommendations.

Ratings: 4 = Excellent 3 = Good 2 = Fair 1 = Needs Improvement				
Attendance/punctuality: Bryce was always 10 minutes early to work and had no absences during the internship.	④	3	2	1
Hygiene: Other than reminding Bryce to clean his glasses before his shift, his hygiene was appropriate for the work environment	④	3	2	1
Response to supervision (from supervisor, coworkers, evaluator): Bryce listened well to his coworkers when they gave him new tasks to complete. He had difficulty asking for new tasks when he finished and did not take the initiative to "find" tasks to do.	4	③	2	1
Ability to follow directions (verbal, written, demonstration, from whom): Bryce followed directions best when the task was demonstrated by his supervisor or coworker and paired with verbal instructions.	4	③	2	1
Tolerance for reinstruction/constructive feedback: Bryce tolerated feedback well if it was brief; too much talking distracted him. If he needed reinstruction on completing a task, it was best to show him and use limited words.	4	③	2	1
Endurance/stamina: Bryce has great endurance and stamina. He worked his 3-hour shift every day and did not seem tired or worn out after work.	④	3	2	1
Ability to meet productivity requirements: Bryce often would exceed the productivity requirements, often finishing his stocking an hour before his shift ended. This is where initiative in finding new tasks to do or asking his supervisor/coworkers for more duties would have helped his performance.	④	3	2	1
Ability to meet quality requirements: Bryce did what he was told and did the job well. However, he did not find tasks to do on his own with regard to keeping the store clean or facing the items on the shelves.	4	3	②	1
Independent/interdependent work ability (completing tasks, asking for assistance): Bryce was very independent, sometimes too independent. He did not ask for assistance when he needed it (e.g., if searching for an item on the shelf for stocking, he would keep walking around the store and often walk past the item several times).	4	3	②	1
Communication (with supervisor, coworkers, customers): Bryce communicated with his coworkers and supervisors only when they spoke to him. Bryce did not initiate conversation or ask questions when he did not understand an assignment. He was friendly to customers but would not initiate (e.g., asking if they needed help, saying hello) and would wait for customers to approach him.	4	3	②	1

(continued)

Figure 5.7. *(continued)* Page 3 of 3

Initiative: This is an area for Bryce to improve on. Once finished with a task, he would wander around the store, not taking the initiative to find other tasks to do (e.g., he could always face items on the shelves but would wait to be told to do so).	4	3	2	(1)
Motivation to work: Bryce is very motivated to work. He stated that he enjoyed this internship because he liked being around people. He also enjoyed getting his paycheck every 2 weeks!	(4)	3	2	1

Learning style (logical/mathematical, visual/spatial, bodily/kinesthetic, musical, interpersonal, intrapersonal): Bodily, kinesthetic, and intrapersonal—Bryce likes to process information provided to him for 2–3 minutes before trying it out on his own.

Adaptations/special equipment needed: An iPod touch might be helpful to remind Bryce of other tasks he could be working on when he finishes an assignment from his supervisor. He could be taught that once he finishes a job, he should look at his iPod touch for other duties to work on.

Strengths displayed during internship: Once Bryce learns the job, he is very efficient. He follows directions well and has great stamina on the job. Bryce was very productive on the job, meeting or exceeding the productivity expectations.

Areas of need displayed during internship: Taking initiative and asking for assistance are the biggest areas to work on. Another area to work on would be initiating communication with supervisor, coworkers, and customers.

Recommendations
(extend work experience, additional work experiences, type of employment, work culture, environment, etc.)

Of the three work experiences Bryce completed, he liked Walgreens the best. He enjoyed the work environment (his coworkers and the customers) and tasks (sitting to price items, standing and walking, working with customers). An employment portfolio that includes the employer evaluations and letters of recommendation along with photos of Bryce doing the various jobs will be put together. Bryce can then go out with his Employment Consultant to talk with businesses about his work and what he would like to do. Working in an environment with a variety of tasks and interactions would be the best for Bryce.

Bryce Johnson _____   _____
Intern Signature   Date

Porter Smith _____   _____
Evaluator Signature   Date

Work experiences or internships are ways for students to experience the world of work under the safety net of the school. When students do well on their internships, employers may want to hire them, which is exactly what we want to happen. It is important that you do not consider the business a "school site," and if an employer wants to hire a student, you should celebrate this achievement!

Adult Service Agency Vignette

Jenny attended an after-hours business event at the local chamber of commerce. During this event, she talked with several employers in the area about their business needs and what they look for in potential employees. Using the business cards she created, she exchanged her cards with the employers she met. After the meeting, she wrote basic information about each employer on the back of the employer's card. The next day, she sent an e-mail to the employers she had met with some individualized information based on their discussion and requesting time to come to their business to discuss more about their business needs. Of the 10 employers she reached out to, five responded offering some dates and times. The other five responded that they were not currently available, so Jenny put their information in her calendar to follow up with them in a month. She followed up with the employers willing to meet with her and scheduled meetings. Her first meeting was at a local retail store. Jenny came 20 minutes early and walked around the store making observations prior to her meeting. She observed that the clothing and shoes were in disarray, clothing was on the floor, sizes were not organized on hangers or in stacks, boxes of shoes were open and strewn on the floor, and shoes were not in correct boxes. She also observed several customers sifting through items and overheard them noting they could not find their size. When she met with the manager, Jenny conducted an informational interview and determined that he could make decisions in his store (versus having to go to corporate to get permission). Jenny asked the manager about the business and how long he had been manager. She talked with the manager about what she had observed and discussed the possibility of having someone organize the clothing and shoes. After the meeting, Jenny wrote a proposal letter identifying a customized job for one of her clients.

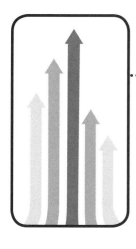

6

Providing Training and Supports While in School and After

Mr. Lewis is the high school special education teacher in his small rural school with additional responsibility for the students enrolled in the 18 to 21 program. He has a good working relationship with the adult services provider in his community, and they actually play basketball on an adult league together. Mr. Lewis is proud of his ability to prepare students for work when they graduate and keeps abreast of their accomplishments through regular communication with his friend. Unfortunately, this small town has a high unemployment rate, so when someone does get a job, it is reason to celebrate.

One of Mr. Lewis's students, Matthew, is 18 years old and has autism. He is well known through his network of family and friends as well as his community-based school experiences. Matthew is articulate, polite, friendly, and passionate about sports. He attends, watches, and reads about sporting events and can cite team and player statistics across all sports. People are drawn to him for the latest news about their favorite teams.

As a result of these relationships, Matthew was offered a job at a local sporting goods store where he would earn $10 an hour and be responsible for straightening and stocking shelves, ordering equipment and merchandise, helping customers, and ringing sales during evening hours and weekends. He told Mr. Lewis he was starting work the following weekend and was excited about all the things he was going to do with his paycheck.

Mr. Lewis knew Matthew had many skills and could communicate well, so people often failed to recognize Matthew's need for individualized training and support. The employer expected Matthew to complete his job duties like any other employee. Mr. Lewis had observed Matthew struggle during his work experience with early morning hours (weekend shifts), responding appropriately when asked to do something he did not know how to do (helping customers), deciding how much stock was available in comparison to what was required to determine need (ordering merchandise), and having a strategy in place at times of great stress and meltdowns.

Mr. Lewis was concerned Matthew would lose his job if appropriate training and supports were not provided. He talked with Matthew and his family, who gave him permission to speak with the employer. He approached the owner of the sporting goods store to introduce himself and explained that Matthew was one of his students and how pleased he was to hear of Matthew's new job. Mr. Lewis reinforced the employer's decision that Matthew would be a valuable employee and stressed all the assets he would bring to the company. He mentioned that he would like to come with Matthew at the beginning to make sure he understood all of his duties and to ensure that he was completing them to the employer's standards. The owner readily agreed and was happy that someone was taking an interest in Matthew and his business.

Mr. Lewis accompanied Matthew on his first few days. He identified the work duties and schedule, developed task analyses for his job duties, observed a coworker whom Matthew seemed to hit it off with who could provide some assistance, and determined a "way out" for Matthew to go to the break room when a 5-minute break was needed. Mr. Lewis went to the job site each day with Matthew until the data indicated he was completing his job, he laid out a follow-along schedule for monitoring Matthew's work performance, and he compiled a list of people to call if a problem occurred. All of this information was shared with the adult services provider who would be responsible for supporting Matthew in his job once he left school.

Good news—a student has just become employed! While this is an exciting time and certainly a reason to celebrate, it is important to remember that getting the job is only the beginning; learning and keeping the job are important considerations that cannot be overlooked. Whether it is a work experience turned into permanent paid employment, a part-time job in the afternoons and on weekends while still enrolled in school, or a job that was found with the help of adult services as the student is exiting school, the teacher plays a critical role in assisting the individual with becoming successful on the job. Assistance may take the form of advocacy, direct instruction, or collaboration.

Remember all of the supports that were implemented for the student while in the classroom and on community work experience sites? Those supports help the student look and be competent, leading to his or her employment. At the same time, they elevate the expectations that he or she can work, and as a result, others often may feel the individual does not need instruction and support to be able to work. It is important to advocate on the individual's behalf to ensure the delivery of essential supports by a skilled person, such as an employment support professional. Sharing information about the individual's support needs and preferences through the use of a portfolio, personal communication, or other form of documentation can be a valuable option. Conducting training together with adult service staff or visiting the jobsite to provide input on instructional techniques and supports can be an effective way to apply your knowledge and expertise in the context of the actual employment situation.

TEACHING SELF-DETERMINATION

Teaching the student self-determination skills while in school prepares him or her to be actively involved in asking for help and communicating support needs. This is a critical skill for the student to ensure that he or she receives ongoing assistance as needed beyond the availability of school personnel. The positive impact of enhanced self-determination for youth with disabilities is evident in the improved adult outcomes that are reported in all areas, including employment (Shogren, 2013; Wehmeyer et al., 2009). Those individuals who exhibit skills associated with self-determination, such as decision making, problem solving, and exercising choice and control, are the ones who are most frequently considered employable and who, as research indicates, experience greater success on the job (Wehmeyer & Parent, 2011).

What about those students who are not displaying those skills or have not yet developed them? Work is one of the key ways students can actually learn self-determination skills. Actively participating in setting goals, choosing a job, asking for accommodations, practicing self-management and following instructions, making decisions on how to complete tasks, and addressing infrequent exceptions to the work schedule are all prime opportunities for learning and practicing self-determination skills. Teaching self-determination indirectly, such as by modeling, and directly, such as with systematic instruction, should be considered an essential component of any vocational and on-the job training (Hughes & Carter, 2012). Students learn best in the environments where they are going to use those skills, and businesses in the community provide a great opportunity to learn and enhance self-determination for all students.

IDENTIFYING INSTRUCTIONAL STRATEGIES AND SUPPORTS

Job placement decisions are based on knowledge of 1) the skills, interests, passions, and support needs of the student and 2) the opportunities and business needs of the employer. No matter how good the job match, gaps that exist must be identified and bridged with the use of training, supports, and accommodations. The repertoire of tools for bridging the gaps includes the following:

- Instructional strategies

- Natural supports and cues

- Assistive technology

- Environmental modifications

- Compensatory strategies

- Employer negotiations

INSTRUCTIONAL STRATEGIES

Once a student has found a job, what are the first steps to get started and plan instruction? As training is begun, an important first step is the development of a *task analysis* to guide instruction. Developing a task analysis before the first day of work can be very helpful but is sometimes not possible and instead must be completed within the first few days on the job. The task analysis is a step-by-step breakdown of the work tasks. The steps should be written as verbal prompts in specific detail so that when followed, the job will be completed. See Figure 6.1 for a task analysis form.

The task analysis is essential for providing training in a consistent way, a critical element to enhance learning. It is also invaluable if more than one person is providing jobsite support, particularly when school and adult service personnel are both involved, to ensure it is delivered in the same way. Another important benefit is data collection as an indicator that learning is taking place and a means to identify areas where additional supports are needed. Without this critical information, a trainer may leave the jobsite too early, jeopardizing the worker's success, or may stay on the jobsite too long without being effective and thereby negatively impacting employer relations.

Building on the task analysis and determining the job duty schedule provides insight into the work requirements and the workplace cultural expectations for the new employee. First, identify all the major tasks and determine a routine that ensures completion, taking into account any factors that need to be considered. Be sure to include arrival at work, breaks, lunch, clocking out, and any other aspects of the individual's entire workday. It is important to be as efficient as possible and to remove any judgment that may be difficult for the individual to differentiate, especially if it is a critical component of the job. For example, discriminating between clean and dirty may present a challenge, but teaching a pattern that always ensures clean no matter how dirty the item is just prevents a potential problem in

Task Analysis

Trainer: _____ Employer: _____

Environment: _____ Work Cue: _____

Key:

+, independent correct response   G, gesture prompt

−, incorrect response   M, model prompt

I, indirect prompt   P, physical prompt

V, verbal prompt

Figure 6.1. Task analysis. (*Source:* Virginia Commonwealth University©, Rehabilitation Research & Training Center on Supported Employment, 2008)

the future. Another critical piece often overlooked is identifying exceptions and changes, such as holidays, seasonal changes, and certain rush hours throughout the day. These should be addressed in the training or included in the follow-along training schedule as the events occur. Thinking through a plan of instruction, supports, and accommodations prior to the first day of work can help ensure a smoother, more effective process with fewer surprises for both the job coach and the student.

A teaching technique known as *systematic instruction*, using the task analysis, offers an effective tool for training the new employee (Gold, 1978; Snell & Brown, 2006; Storey & Miner, 2011). Begin by recording each step of the task analysis on the Task Analysis form. Instruction is provided for each step of the task analysis using a system of least prompts, which means starting with the least intrusive one, waiting 3–5 seconds before introducing the next level of prompting, and continuing until the individual completes the step. These include indirect, verbal, gesture, modeling, and physical. On the Task Analysis form, jot down the level of prompting required for the step, indicated by I (indirect), V (verbal), G (gesture), M (model), or P (physical). This recording method provides training data so you can see that learning is taking place, particularly if the individual has not yet mastered the skill but requires a lesser prompt to perform the task. Documenting a plus (+) or minus (−) allows the gathering of probe data as an indication of overall performance. It is recommended that probe data be collected once a week and training data once a day.

Once the task analysis is completed, decisions about how the individual will be taught for the new job must be thoughtfully planned. The Instructional Plan can be a useful tool to think about how best to do this (Figure 6.2). The information gathered during classroom and community-based instruction is likely to have generated ideas of the most effective teaching techniques that the new employee will learn from. Maybe the student responded best to verbal instruction, perhaps she became agitated when physically prompted, or maybe he did not attend to the task, so gesturing was ineffective.

It is important to include reinforcement when the individual completes the desired steps. Verbal praise is the most common form and one that is most likely to be maintained by the environment after the job coach or trainer is gone. Making statements that repeat the desired behavior, such as "Nice job working fast," "I like the way you kept working while you greeted your supervisor," and "That's the way we pick up the box," offer an additional opportunity for indirect instruction.

NATURAL SUPPORTS

All employees rely on support from others with some aspect of their jobs. Whether it is a morning wake-up call, a reminder to do something, or an offer of assistance, people come to rely on and/or enjoy the helpful gestures from others. People with disabilities are no different, and their presence on the jobsite opens doors for new relationships and for people to extend a hand. Often, the demonstration by a job coach is helpful to facilitate interactions, especially if people have little or no experience with persons who have a disability. Others often just figure out on their own how best to communicate and provide assistance. For example, Harry was a young man who sustained a traumatic brain injury and physical complications from an auto accident that occurred during his senior year in high school. He became employed at a large department store, sorting and preparing clothes for hanging in their respective departments. His mother drove him to and from work and also assisted him with walking through the store to his workstation in the back. The coworkers befriended Harry, and one approached the job coach and asked why Harry's mother walked Harry to

Instructional Plan

Placement Information:

Individual Name: _____ Start Date: _____

Employment Specialist/Job Coach: _____

Name of Company: _____ Position: _____

Supervisor: _____ Salary: _____ Hours: _____

Schedule: _____

Job Duties: _____

Preparation Activities Completed (Please check all that apply):
- ❏ Assessment/Discovery
- ❏ Job Analysis
- ❏ Task Analysis (Please attach to Instructional Plan)

Training Schedule:

Days and hours: _____

Potential gaps or issues to be addressed: _____

_____

Estimated time period for training: _____

Brief explanation/justification: _____

Instructional Strategies:

Prompting techniques: _____

_____

Reinforcement strategies: _____

_____

Compensatory strategies: _____

_____

Other assistive technology, jobsite modifications, or supports: _____

_____

Data Collection Procedures:

Task analysis	On task
Production	Other _____

Performance Criteria (For example, 3 days at 100% on task analysis):

_____

Problem-Solving Provisions (If criteria are not met or other unanticipated issues occur):

_____

_____

Fading Schedule (Preliminary schedule for fading instruction and time on the jobsite):

_____

_____

Vocational Rehabilitation Provisions:

Method and frequency of communication: _____

Reporting requirements: _____

Provisions for modifying plan: _____

Comments:

_____

Completed By: _____ **Date:** _____

Figure 6.2. Instructional plan.

his workstation each day. She said that she and her coworkers help Harry through the day and were happy to meet him at the door in the mornings and escort him out in the evenings. The natural relationships that developed extended to an essential support needed for Harry. It is likely that the same outcome might not have occurred if coworkers were directly asked to perform this support or if Harry's job were contingent upon this offer of support in order to be successful.

This example highlights some critical considerations when thinking about the provision of natural supports. Often, in developing a plan for a student's upcoming employment, a job coach or other employment support personnel will say, "We are going to use natural supports." It is important to remember that natural supports are just that—*natural*—so they need time to develop and emerge, but people have to be in the actual work environment in order for natural supports to form. First, one support is not enough. Think about all the provisions of support that a job coach provides for each person; natural supports can address some of those or parts of an overall support; however, expecting a coworker with his or her own job to become a job coach for the worker not only is unrealistic but also becomes very artificial. The job coach plays a critical role in ensuring all training and support needs are addressed, including those relying on natural supports to ensure that the worker's and employer's needs are responded to.

Second, breakdowns can occur in getting from point A to point B. Just because the employee needs help and a coworker seems willing, the connection to make it happen often needs a little coaxing. For example, a young man with cerebral palsy became employed in an office as a computer programmer. He needed help with lunch every day and welcomed coworkers to assist him. The job coach noticed how friendly the coworkers were and assumed that lunch arrangements would be worked out. Much to the job coach's surprise, the employee missed lunch because no one initiated eating together. The job coach facilitated the employee asking and the coworkers' response and joined them until it became a regular part of the lunch routine.

Third, people like and dislike different things. Some workers may not like coworkers providing assistance or may prefer only males or only females, people of a certain age, or people with other characteristics. The point is that natural supports are individualized. Think about your own job: if someone offers to help and you dislike that person, you may graciously decline. For example, a young woman needed help remembering to complete some of her infrequent job tasks. The job coach asked a male coworker who worked in close proximity to remind the employee when she needed to do them. He was surprised when he checked in for a follow-along visit that the employer expressed concern that these specific tasks were not getting done. The coworker assured the job coach that he was reminding the worker, but he stated that she did not respond to his prompts. When asked, the employee said she did not like her coworker telling her what to do, so she refused to do those tasks. The job coach implemented a checklist and technology with an alarm that enabled the worker to manage her own job duties with great success.

Fourth, natural supports are not a replacement for the old "place and pray" philosophy. Nor are they the panacea to bridge every gap that requires training and instruction. Natural supports are the added benefit we all experience as a result of the relationships we develop with others. While we welcome their use to enrich the employment situation, it is important not to lose sight of the reason supports are needed in the first place. Safeguards and checks and balances need to be put in place to ensure that an essential function is not overlooked because of a breakdown or change in the natural support arrangement.

Assistive Technology

Assistive technology can be useful in assisting the individual and should always be a consideration. These technologies can include mainstream devices, such as an iPod touch, iPad, or smartphone. The iPod touch has been found to be very successful for providing a task analysis and/or videos for the individual to follow. Not only are these tools relatively inexpensive and easily accessible, they are pretty cool and extremely inviting to many users. An added benefit of these devices is that, because the general public also uses them, they can be a common bond connecting the worker with a coworker who is likely to be able to provide assistance if needed.

In addition, these devices offer a means for communication and apps with even more options for support. Examples include Proloquo2Go, GoTalk NOW, TalkTablet, and iCommunicate for augmentative and alternative communication and Time Timer, Voice Reminders!, Dragon Dictation, and Work System to assist with remembering, organizing, and reminding. Most jobsites now require the use of computers. Teaching the student to use them at work is essential. Important computer-based activities include communicating by e-mail, having a color-coded daily work schedule saved online, accessing important information at work, and just being a part of the gang with listserv messages sent to all employees.

For example, Ralph had a learning disability, traumatic brain injury, and chronic health issues. He would miss a lot of time from school and get behind on his assignments, which increased his stress. Interestingly, as a result, his IEP team felt that he would not be able to manage college or a job. His teacher would review his missed work and assignments upon his return. An iPod touch was introduced to enable Ralph to keep track of his work, and he was given a calendar so he could assign missed work over a period of time and stay current with his new assignments. Perhaps most important, Ralph was taught to ask his teachers what he had missed and to negotiate late due dates. His anxiety was reduced, his grades improved, and he actually missed fewer days. Ralph also learned self-management and communication skills essential for achieving his postsecondary goals. After graduating, Ralph attended community college for 2 years and found a job as an assistant with an architectural firm, continuing to use his iPod touch in both environments.

Environmental Modifications

Another option is a job modification, for example, changing the sequence of job duties or moving the workstation to avoid a potential problem or distraction. Any changes to the job environment should be in the least disruptive way possible and made with the employer's approval. Often, a task is completed a certain way because that is the way it has always been done. Employers are frequently amenable to workers' requests for change, and the change might offer improved performance or better conditions for all employees. It is not uncommon for an employer to comment, "This was helpful for all my employees."

Moving someone's workspace to a private location, turning a desk around so a person's back is to the line of traffic, altering the sequence of work duties to avoid the customer rush, changing a script for customer service to ensure all important information is introduced, and changing a work schedule to accommodate transportation demands are just a few examples of changes that might be requested and implemented. Flexible work hours and telecommuting are common perks for the general workforce that can be helpful to an employee with a disability.

The following two scenarios demonstrate other ways an employer might accommodate a worker:

Naomi's mental health issues often made it difficult for her to physically be in the office, so it was arranged for her to call in and work from home on those days.

Malcolm had "bad days" and lost several jobs because he missed work on those days or was belligerent and disruptive if he went to work. He became employed at a restaurant, and it was negotiated that he would have one weekend and a few extra days off each month. His monthly schedule was put on a calendar so that when Malcolm felt like he could not go to work, he could pull up his calendar and see with relief that he had a day off soon. The calendar was a productive solution for Malcolm's frustration and preferences, and it helped his employers and coworkers to understand Malcolm better since he was nonverbal and unable to communicate feelings directly.

Rehabilitation engineering can be brought in to build modifications that can solve a problem. For example, building a divided cart for organizing deliveries, creating an accessible workstation, and designing a platform for use with a wheelchair can make an individual's job easier. Rehabilitation engineering services can often be accessed through the state vocational rehabilitation office or a university engineering department. These specialists can assist with designing, developing, adapting, and applying technology to address problems experienced by individuals with disabilities. It is suggested that their services be consulted to visit the jobsite, assess the problem, and build or modify a solution. For example, Susan was hired in the medical records department and had difficulty keeping track of the order of documents and folders to be filed. Rehabilitation engineering designed and built a mobile cart with vertical alphabetical slots that she could use to sort documents and move to the desired filing area, which both increased her speed and improved her accuracy. Similarly, a young man with a traumatic brain injury and limited mobility was assisted by rehabilitation engineering personnel who adapted his workstation to make it the correct height and added an individually designed sorting and hanging rack so he could complete his job as soft line merchandise assistant in a major department store.

Deciding which strategies to use can be based on assessment information. A behavior or support need observed in one environment may not be necessary in another, so it is important to be prepared according to the information you have gathered. Being proactive is the key. For example, if you know there is potential for issues on the job, by all means implement one of the strategies found to be most successful. Including the strategy in the task analysis and providing instruction using the technique is likely to reduce valuable training time later. A common mistake is to wait and implement a compensatory strategy or assistive technology only as a last resort. One recommendation is to try something early on to enhance the learning process and individual performance. It is always easier to take something away at a later time if it is not needed.

Thinking through the training before the job starts and finalizing it soon after enables the job coach to be better prepared and enhances his or her effectiveness. The first few days are always hectic, as the job coach is trying to make sure the job gets done while conveying an image of the new employee's competence to the employer and coworkers. It is well known that the more changes that are made, the greater the potential for increased training time as the mistake or new way of doing it is retaught. Not every change can be avoided, but the more planning that is done upfront, the more successful the worker will be and the faster the job coach will be able to fade from the jobsite.

Despite our best laid plans, challenges can occur on the job. Perhaps the individual has learned all but a few steps, or can perform the task but not at a competitive rate, or has exhibited an infrequent but disruptive behavior, or can do the job but is having difficulty at break and interacting with coworkers. As such issues are noticed, it is important to include strategies for addressing them in training through instruction, compensatory strategies, or another behavioral intervention. One desired technique is to include a "way out" for the worker, teaching an acceptable response to stress or anger, such as taking a break, making a phone call, or having a backup enjoyable and calming work task to do.

Compensatory Strategies

During initial and ongoing training, it is important to consider the use of compensatory strategies, such as a checklist, an alarm watch, a picture book, or a timer. Think about the multiple reminders we all use for ourselves in a job. Perhaps we make a list, jot down on a Post-it Note, set a watch alarm, or use online calendar notifications. Many of the individuals we are helping to get employed may not have experience in using these tools, or if they have used them, they may have difficulty reading a new situation and generalizing their use in a different environment. It is up to the person providing jobsite support to think about potential areas that may need reminding and to implement strategies that reduce the amount of judgment a worker needs to make. As a teacher, whether you or someone else is providing jobsite training, sharing information about the kinds of areas that the individual may need help with and the compensatory strategies you have found useful in the past is a valuable contribution.

For example, consider Nathan, who completed his community work experience at a grocery store. He did a great job, but when he saw someone he knew, Nathan would get distracted, stop to talk with the person, and forget what he was doing. As a result, he would stand there unable to remember his task and complete his assigned work. His supervisor gave high accolades about Nathan's customer service, so removing his interactions was not an option. Instead, the teacher decided to use a checklist of Nathan's job duties each day. When Nathan moved to a task, he would put a checkmark beside it so he knew what he was working on. When he completed it, he would scratch through the task. Using a laminated chart with a dry erase marker allowed Nathan to wipe his checklist at the end of the day in preparation for his next day's routines. When Nathan graduated and was referred to adult services, this information accompanied him as an important strategy to use on his permanent job.

Compensatory strategies can take many forms. It is best to implement a tangible reminder to replace the abstract remembering of an important work responsibility. If the employer wants the mail delivered at a certain time, all trash cans to be emptied when half full, or a particular task completed once a week, it is important to ensure that these requests from the employer are met. As the worker becomes acclimated to the jobsite and fits in to the workplace culture, it is likely that coworker and other interruptions will become an invited part of the workday.

As natural occurrences increase in the work environment, chances of forgetting an infrequent but important task mount. It is always best to put a reminder in place and much easier to remove or ignore it if it is not needed. Think about Marilyn, who worked in an office. It was a pet peeve of her employer to have the mail put into the incorrect mailbox. Since Marilyn could not read the names on the front of the box, her job coach put name cues on the inside of each person's mailbox. Consider Jimmy, who worked in a legal office and had trouble navigating special orders on the copy machine, so multiple color-coded cues were placed on the copier along with a mini cheat sheet to guide him through remembering the infrequent requests correctly. Other examples include tape on a wall to indicate daily productivity rates, color-coded shelves for organizing supplies, pictures to reinforce written messages, and a laminated food preparation list with items and amount options for the supervisor to circle each day.

Employer Negotiations

Once on the job, aspects of the position often are found to be less than conducive for the new employee. Many of these issues are best addressed by making changes to the position or environment. For example, Tory had a laundry position folding towels, and at certain times of the day when the housekeepers came in to reload their linens, she was distracted watching them and stopped folding while they were present. A conversation with the supervisor identified the option of moving her workstation to face away from the line of traffic so that Tory would not be tempted to stop and stare; Tory's work productivity was thereby improved. Another worker, responsible for cleaning rooms in a school, had difficulty completing his work once the spring weather began. Observation and data indicated that he was distracted by the students on the playground, so a restructured duty schedule was proposed to his supervisor, who agreed to the change.

Jonathan worked for an architecture office and would complete most of his duties but could be found talking frequently to coworkers during afternoon data entry, slowing himself and coworkers down. The employer asked Jonathan's job coach to come and discuss the problem and suggested a change in office space for the data entry task and an added break when the task is completed, giving Jonathan more time to socialize with coworkers. Talking with the employer may result in options that were not considered and offer a more effective alternative to the problem. While small changes may not seem to impact the workplace, it is important to discuss the proposed change with the employer, obtain the employer's approval, and ensure that the change has no unintended consequences. In addition, you will want to make sure that the coworkers and supervisor are aware of changes in routine so that they are informed when working together and responding to the employee's questions.

Responding to Work-Related and Social Issues

An important and often overlooked responsibility is teaching work-related behaviors. It is not uncommon for an individual to know how to do the job but to lose it over workplace behavior requirements and expectations. Be sure to include training in areas such as grooming, taking breaks, interacting with coworkers, participating in company-sponsored activities, and being a good coworker. While training is being provided, students will be watching the trainer to learn how to interact with and involve the individual. Facilitating this process is one of the job coach's critical roles. Do not assume that the individual can read the culture of the workplace and respond accordingly without assistance. The use of training tools to ensure the worker demonstrates social and work-related skills is critical for his or her job success. So how can this be done? First, get a read of the workplace culture beginning with the job analysis. Ask the supervisor and observe others to get a broad perspective. For example, one CEO of a company boasted during the job analysis that all of his employees were like one big, happy family. After talking with the frontline supervisor and observing coworkers, the job coach discovered that not only were they not friends but the employees disliked one another. Think about the impact on the job match and the instruction offered to the student in these very different scenarios.

Remember with all new jobs, a new employee has an initial impression of the workplace that evolves over time as they become more familiar with the environment. It is important that workers with disabilities learn these unwritten rules to the workplace culture and how to respond accordingly. For example, one restaurant owner expected all of his employees to greet him a certain way when he entered—a vital requirement that the employee failed to recognize and almost lost her job as a consequence. Consider the workplace where the expectation is to bring a treat to put in the break room and the negative impact that would have on the employee who did not pick up on that unspoken rule yet enjoyed the snacks others brought. How about the legal assistant who interrupted the legal secretaries and attorneys every time he had a question, not realizing that an open door policy was not literally an open door policy until his disruptions almost cost him his job.

Think about Selena, well known for her sense of humor, who was employed at a bank and over time became disliked by everyone; she was written up to be terminated because of her habit of going daily to her coworkers' offices—no matter how busy they were—and telling them the *same joke*. It is important to observe the expectations and to monitor changes over time, as coworkers and supervisors change often, affecting the overall atmosphere of the workplace. It is not unusual for a worker to not read or to ignore these changes without job coach assistance. This illustrates the importance of natural supports, as that person within the workplace is the best one to share with the employee what he or she should do. The extreme importance of social skills and the compelling evidence suggesting that many jobs are lost because of poor social skills strengthens the argument that these are essential elements for the job coach to address and must not be left to chance.

Modeling is an effective way to teach many social skills and should be demonstrated by the job coach at all times. For example, a job coach texted on her phone while providing training at a company where the use of cell phones was prohibited; no wonder, after she faded from the jobsite, she received a call that the worker was in trouble for texting on his phone while at his desk working. Other social and work-related skills may need direct instruction using the task analysis prompting, reinforcement, and data collection strategies to teach and monitor performance.

Finally, learning these social skills should not be delayed until employment but should be a part of every school day and work experience. Think about the student whom everyone hugs and who is allowed to not follow appropriate social distances during her school day because "she doesn't know any better": she will likely continue this inappropriate behavior at her place of employment. Another student pushed a fellow student into the lockers, and instead of using it as a teaching moment and having him stop and apologize, his aide rushed him to the classroom. His opportunities to be integrated with his peers were reduced even further. The more trials that students with disabilities have, the more experiences they get with their peers without disabilities; the more they are held accountable to the same expectations that others are held to, the better they will be at developing and demonstrating essential social skills enhancing their inclusion in the workplace and other environments. Some ideas that can go a long way on the jobsite include 1) asking others how they are doing, 2) paying someone a compliment, 3) offering assistance, 4) maintaining personal hygiene (e.g., wearing deodorant, brushing teeth), 5) looking good (wearing stylish clothes, having a nice haircut), 6) initiating greetings, and 7) asking for more work.

Implementing Provisions for Job Retention

From day one, it is important to start thinking about leaving the jobsite. The task analysis and other types of training data (e.g., production, social interactions, and behavioral incidents) allow decisions to be made based on what the data is telling you. If the individual has mastered a task according to all of the steps performed with 100% accuracy, typically for three days, then you will want to reduce your presence while that task is being performed. One common technique is to move across the room for several days and then into another area,

Fading Plan

Placement Information:

Individual Name: _____ Start Date: _____

Employment Specialist/Job Coach: _____

Name of Company: _____ Position: _____

Supervisor: _____ Salary: _____ Hours: _____

Schedule: _____

Job Duties: _____

Fading from the Work Area:

Work tasks: _____

Fading schedule: _____

Data monitoring procedures: _____

Continued areas of instruction: _____

Fading from the Job Site:

Days and hours: _____

Fading schedule: _____

Data monitoring procedures: _____

Estimated time period for fading: _____

Brief explanation/justification: _____

_____

Follow-Along Support:

_____

_____

Completed By: _____ **Date:** _____

Figure 6.3. Fading plan. (*Source*: Creative Employment Opportunities, Inc., Milwaukee, WI).

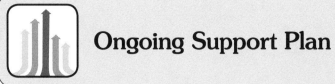

Ongoing Support Plan

Date: _____

Name: _____ Company: _____

Days/Hours a Week; _____ Funding Source: _____

Long-Term Goal (e.g., In 6 months, Jenny will increase her independence by taking the initiative and completing tasks as they come up):

_____

_____

_____

_____

Short-Term Objectives (e.g., Jenny will use her checklist to identify tasks that should be completed during her shift. Jenny will ask her supervisor or coworker for additional work when she has completed her work):

_____

_____

_____

_____

Action Plan to Achieve Goals/Objectives:

_____

_____

_____

_____

Progress Made Toward Goals (update at team meeting):

_____

_____

_____

_____

Figure 6.4. Ongoing support plan. (*Source*: Creative Employment Opportunities, Inc., Milwaukee, WI).

out of sight, for another several days, continuing to record data upon your return. If performance is maintained without the trainer's presence, as indicated by the data and employer feedback, fading can continue and begin offsite during those times. Be sure to reinforce the employee for doing such a good job working independently.

The fading process is likely to be staggered across tasks and times of day, as certain activities are mastered while others are in varying levels of instruction. It is important to ensure that the performance criteria have been met before fading decisions are made. A fading plan will provide critical information to share with the team, who can monitor changes outside of the job that can impact work or are a result of work so that they can be proactively addressed (Figure 6.3).

As time is reduced on the job, establishing a mechanism of communication with adult services and everyone's role in providing ongoing support is essential. Developing an ongoing support plan that highlights the individual's potential needs, options for addressing them, person responsible for overseeing, and details about arranging is an important strategy to ensure that everyone is aware and ready to respond as the need arises (Figure 6.4). It is important to note that, by definition, individuals receiving supported employment services receive a minimum of two visits a month to monitor their success on the job. Ongoing supports should be individualized on the basis of the current and potential needs of the individual. A critical element for job retention is the provision of ongoing follow-along supports. A common mistake is for the student to be working well when he or she graduates from school, so linking with adult services is often overlooked. No matter where the individual is in the employment process or how long he or she has been working while in school, the need for supports and accommodations is essential and should not be overlooked. Detailed communication by the teacher and the sharing of relevant employment data can ensure that the success experienced while in school continues into adulthood.

SUMMARY

It is an exciting time when an individual gets hired, and it is easy to think "my work is done." However, ensuring supports and accommodations are in place for job success is important. As an educator, you are skilled at providing instructional techniques and knowledgeable of strategies that were effective for the new employee while in the classroom. Implementing supports such as compensatory strategies and assistive technology can help the individual to perform his or her job at the quality and rate expected by the employer. Facilitating natural supports is important for building relationships on and off the job that can be essential for performance and critical for establishing friendships. Teaching self-determination skills and assisting the student with understanding his or her preferred supports and how to request them on the job is helpful for greater independence and job retention. An important role is to advocate on behalf of the student to facilitate community and adult service supports to ensure their availability for long-term employment assistance, success, and advancement.

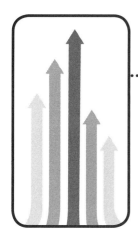

7

Ways to Overcome the *Yeah, but . . .* Syndrome

Maria is a young woman who has volunteered at the local hospital and worked at a restaurant for more than 10 years until she was laid off. For the past 3 years, she has worked as an administrative assistant at a local school district where she assists others with various clerical duties (assembling folders and individualized education program [IEP] packets, stuffing envelopes for mailings, creating name badges, shredding, etc.). Now close your eyes and picture Maria at work. What does she look like? What skills does she have? What type of disability do you envision Maria having? How do you perceive Maria? Would you be surprised to know that Maria has a visual impairment? That her records also indicate that she has an intellectual disability? That she experiences seizures and has limited use of her right side and hand? That she has lived in large residential settings and attended segregated classrooms? Fortunately for Maria she attended a public school and had a teacher who believed in her abilities. Her teacher developed a tactile communication system for Maria, took her into the community to develop her work and social skills, and ensured her inclusion in her high school. After graduation, Maria's teacher became her guardian and assisted in moving her out of the residential facility and into the community, where she began working with an adult services agency who also believed in Maria's abilities. Through a lot of trial and error, multiple work experiences, and connecting Maria to her community, Maria was able to secure employment in the community.

Have you ever looked at someone with your eyes but seen them with your mind? Often, this is what happens when we work with individuals with significant disabilities. This is not because we are "bad" people but rather because we are human beings. Do you ever wonder why we often think of the worst-case scenario or what can go wrong instead of thinking about what could go right? In psychological terms, we all are the victims of negative bias (Crawford & Cacioppo, 2002; Rozin & Royzman, 2001). Negative bias is a result of our fight-or-flight response that is activated during negative experiences. The human brain focuses more on negative than positive experiences because negative events often lead to danger. As a result, our brain often alerts itself to potential threats, which cause positive thoughts to take more effort. When we become hyperfocused on the negative, we have a hard time seeing, hearing, or feeling positive. The good news is that we can interrupt this negative bias. As educators, our first priority is to make every effort to counteract negative thoughts and focus on what can happen rather than what cannot happen. The question should not be "Can this student work?" but "How can we help this student work?"

While negative experiences are often unavoidable, reframing or reinterpreting the negative situation in a more positive or even humorous way counters the adverse psychological effects that would otherwise be experienced (Force, 2018).

How can we counteract negative bias? There are three steps educators can take: 1) Take action, because actions will help shift your focus. 2) Provide opportunities for students in a variety of settings. Experiences help shift our focus to what can be. 3) Reframe, reassess, and reevaluate the situation. Find possibilities that can happen; find the value in all experiences, and learn from mistakes. Raise your expectations for yourself and your students. If you believe in the possibilities, then failure is nothing more than a rehearsal for success!

Have you been in presentations where the presenter provides strategies and examples of ways to overcome challenges or your negative bias? It is easy to walk away from these situations thinking, "Yes, but my students are . . . ," and think the information shared may not be relevant for you. No one knows your particular situation, but if you keep an open mind, it is possible to see problems in a different way that may lend itself to new solutions. This chapter helps you look at ways to reframe the situation, ask different questions, and come up with alternative solutions. We often need to think differently and more creatively (e.g., like an advertising agency that has to come up with a new ad campaign for a well-known product). We need to find new ways to address some of our old challenges. As Winston Churchill stated, "A pessimist sees the difficulty in every opportunity. An optimist sees the opportunity in every difficulty."

As you move forward to provide employment services, it is not uncommon to encounter a variety of situations that may appear to be potential roadblocks. For example, an individual may say he or she does not want to work, there may be fears of losing benefits, or family members may have concerns about work. Individuals may present challenging behaviors, lack job skills, or have no work experience. They may be considered not able or not ready to go to work because of a severe disability. Many teachers and service providers will comment that there are no jobs available, employers will not hire, or there is a lack of resources to fund employment services. It can feel overwhelming. As a result, our response is often to approach the situation developmentally. In other words, we place the emphasis on the individual having to "be ready" to go to work and focus on preemployment activities or require him or her to change or do something before being considered employable. For example, it may be felt that the individual needs to learn to write his or her name, to not yell when asked to change a routine, to be able to stay on task until completed, or to meet a specified production rate before employment is considered. It is this sequence of arbitrary criteria that often limits and excludes many individuals from ever getting a job. For example, we may feel that an individual works too slowly, is unable to communicate, has a disheveled appearance, or can perform only one task; however, these assumptions are often not based on the reality of the business market. When we are out in the community visiting businesses, developing relationships, and exploring employers' needs, we may find out that what the employer is looking for is quite different from our assumptions and actually the person is a good match to that individualized situation. For example, a car dealership was having the mechanic clean the car after it was fixed, which was time consuming and costly. A more efficient solution was discovered by hiring a worker with a disability who wanted to perform the same single task all day, which freed up the mechanic to repair more cars.

Think about how different the situation is if we approach it from an employment first perspective. What if we start with employment and look at what the individual's assets and contributions are? Instead of determining if this person can work, we start from the point of reference that the individual is going to work and it is up to us to figure out how. We are basically flipping the glass from being a negative half empty to a positive half full. For example, a situational assessment was being conducted for a young man with a traumatic brain injury. His teacher commented that he would never work because he was too slow, could not remember next steps, and was easily distracted. When technical assistance was provided to include systematic instruction for the student, it was found that he responded best to modeling prompts, and with multiple trials he was able to remember the task and actually worked at a competitive rate, changing the teacher's perspective on this young man's employability. Looking at the situation differently offers the opportunity to focus on solutions. Another example is an individual who wanted to work but was not considered for employment because he had no transportation. A good job match was found, and training on riding a bicycle to and from work was brainstormed and became the creative solution. It is important to remember that everyone on the young adult's team may have a different perspective and is using that lens in making his or her determination about employment. Taking the lead, demonstrating an employment first perspective, advocating on behalf of the individual, and promoting creative brainstorming are all important actions that can be taken and have a profound impact on reframing the situation and influencing the employment outcome.

Let's take a look at some examples and think about ways to rephrase the situations.

CASE STUDY: STUDENT HAS POOR HYGIENE Jesus is a 16-year-old young man very interested in getting a job. He has had a goal to improve his hygiene for the past 3 years. Jesus has been told by his teachers that until his hygiene improves, he cannot get a job. He has been given a morning routine checklist that he needs to bring in each day (brush teeth, shower, wash hair, use deodorant), but he routinely fails to bring in the checklist or brings it in with only one or two items checked.

What questions can you ask?

- Why are our instructional strategies not working?
- What alternative instructional strategies could be used?
- Why does the student not understand the need for good hygiene?

How can this situation be reframed?

Instead of focusing on poor hygiene, ask, Are there jobs where hygiene is not an issue? At the same time, Jesus should still have the goal of maintaining at least some basic hygiene practices.

What else would you do?

Brainstorm ideas with other teachers, friends, and family members. The process of brainstorming requires us to think creatively—individuals should think out loud and suggest as many ideas as possible, no matter how outlandish or bizarre the idea might be. After the list is generated, then begin to analyze and discuss the ideas. From there, you can evaluate and prioritize and disregard solutions that do not make sense (but be sure to think about why they do not make sense) for the situation. That does not mean that poor hygiene is ignored and not still worked on but rather it is no longer a prerequisite before employment is considered.

Explain what happened to Jesus.

The team brainstormed places where hygiene might not matter in a job setting that could potentially be a good job match for Jesus and he could begin employment while continuing to learn better hygiene skills. Interestingly, coworkers can be the best teachers and influence new employees on how best to present themselves for work each day. Here is a general list of what the team generated: garbage collector, city dump, cleaning bathrooms at a rest stop, off-shore oil rig worker, porta-potty cleaner, sewer worker, coal miner, crime/accident scene cleaner, diaper service worker, road kill worker, worm dung farmer—the list went on! As a result of this brainstorming, a local recycling company was identified. Jesus's summer internship led to a 30-hour a week position in the company.

CASE STUDY: STUDENT HAS UNREALISTIC GOALS   Rubin's career goal is to be a rap artist—his favorite artist is Tupac Shakur (Rubin was shot and is now in a wheelchair). Rubin has difficulty in his academic classes and spends most of his time in the hallways at the school. He does not see the connection between his career goal and what he is learning in school.

What questions can you ask?

- Why is Rubin interested in being a rap artist?
- What skills does Rubin have that might lead to a career in this industry?
- What makes this goal unrealistic (be specific)?
- What about the music industry is appealing to Rubin?

How can this situation be reframed?

Use this as an opportunity to teach self-advocacy and self-reflection. Set up an experience (if you can) in the area of interest and have Rubin reflect on what he liked and did not like. Ask what steps he would take to reach his goal—starting with the overall goals, what short-term steps would he need to take to reach that goal? If the goal is something not attainable in your area (e.g., being a rap star), go to the local college/university or high school and have the student interview/talk with the music or band teacher. Have him research the career path of other rap stars. Talk with Rubin about other options along with the goal. He can still pursue the goal, but you can help him pursue something to pay the bills.

What else would you do?

The team brainstormed ideas about how Rubin could explore the rap music world and build connections with others interested in similar music. They thought about music stores, concert venues, radio stations, local band performances, rap artist contacts, high school musicians, and local college programs. A plan was set up for Rubin to visit these settings and talk with people to begin to understand what he would have to do to become a rap artist, and as he became immersed in that world, Rubin learned about other opportunities in the industry and began developing important relationships to help him get connected.

Explain what happened to Rubin.

After researching the rap industry, Rubin agreed to take an English class focusing on poetry writing. At first, he did not want to do this, but he agreed after it was explained that rap music really was poetry. The art teacher's husband was a musician and had his own studio where musicians from the area created their demos. Rubin met with Randy, who talked with him about the ins and outs of the music business. Randy connected him with another studio that worked with musicians in the hip hop/rap industry. Rubin participated in a summer work experience with this studio and was connected to a business that created demo CDs for various local artists. Rubin began working at this company, where he packaged the CDs for local artists, and he continues to hang out at the studio from time to time. While at the CD company, Rubin also connected with local artists. Recently, he went with one of the artists to distribute the artist's CDs to the local radio stations in the area. The demo CD business hired Rubin part time during the school year, and Rubin continues to write his songs and spend time with the musicians from the studio and CD company. He has developed a strong network of local musicians who review his songs and share a common creative bond with him.

CASE STUDY: WE HAVE NO TRANSPORTATION OR RESOURCES FOR COMMUNITY WORK EXPERIENCES   Nikki is an 18-year-old senior who has been diagnosed with autism. She and her family are interested in her working and would like for her to gain experience while in school. The teacher is concerned because there is no public transportation, and the school bus is not available to use to travel to jobsites. In addition, the teacher has no financial assistance to cover any costs associated with the work experience or to pay student wages. She has decided that she will provide an in-school experience in the cafeteria and refer Nikki to adult services for employment when she graduates.

What questions can you ask?

- What other transportation options are available?
- What businesses offer carpooling for employees?
- Who are neighbors and friends that could assist Nikki back and forth to work?
- How does Nikki get around the community now?

How can this situation be reframed?

One option is to facilitate community conversations by bringing the community together to discuss ideas around transition.

Transportation alternatives such as Uber or Lyft can be explored or collaborating with other organizations that provide transportation (i.e., using a local church van) may provide a solution.

What else would you do?

The team met and started thinking about solutions, beginning with how other people get to work without public transportation. A suggestion was made to conduct a community analysis, riding around in Nikki's neighborhood to find out firsthand all the potential options for transportation support that she already used for other purposes. The school and vocational rehabilitation professionals began discussions on how they might be able to work together to fund a work experience and/or paid job during Nikki's school year. The team brainstormed ideas for businesses that would be of interest to Nikki and laid out a plan for job development to explore the transportation options associated with each one, particularly those offered by the company or used by employees of the company.

Explain what happened to Nikki.

The teacher visited Nikki's community and found out that a neighbor drove Nikki to church and a relative often gave Nikki a ride to the mall and other places. She began job development and found a work experience near Nikki's house in a library, where Nikki restocked books and managed online accounts—exactly what she was interested in. The neighbor and relative provided transportation on a regular schedule, with one driving Nikki to work and the other picking her up and taking her to school to complete the rest of her day. Shifting the work experience to begin from her home not only opened new doors but also was more relevant, as that is where Nikki's workday will begin once she graduates and becomes employed.

CASE STUDY: STUDENT'S DISABILITY IS TOO SEVERE—TOO MANY BARRIERS TO EMPLOYMENT   Tiana uses a wheelchair for mobility, has a visual impairment, has limited verbal skills, and has an intellectual disability. She attends a segregated class at her high school where she is focusing on life skills. School and adult services evaluation criteria for determining eligibility have deemed Tiana's disability "too severe," and Tiana is consequently deemed "not ready to work."

What questions can you ask?

- Why are strategies to teach skills not working?
- What instructional strategies and supports would be helpful?
- What are Tiana's unique talents that she contributes to a workplace?
- What does Tiana like to do, and what does she already do in other environments?

How can this situation be reframed?

Conduct situational assessments in real business settings to determine Tiana's functional skills. Spend time with Tiana outside of school, and see whom she spends time with. What does she do outside of school? What does she enjoy? Complete a community map, develop business relationships, and visit local companies to determine various job requirements. Revisit Tiana's educational program, explore opportunities for learning that are relevant to work, and involve her with her fellow students without disabilities.

What else would you do?

Tiana lived in a group home, so the teacher interviewed the staff and spent time with Tiana in the home. She saw that Tiana was very outgoing, always smiling, and wanted to be helpful. The teacher found out key information that included the fact that Tiana's day consisted of going to school and then going home. She did not have any connections outside of those two worlds. While at the group home, the teacher noticed that Tiana enjoyed watching the group home staff at work in the kitchen, though Tiana watched from the kitchen door because of the size of her wheelchair. The teacher completed a community map to determine what types of businesses were within a 1- to 2-mile radius of where Tiana lived. She invited several of the local businesses to her business advisory committee meeting (a bimonthly meeting with local businesses, hosted by a business that worked with her students, to discuss employment for her students). The manager of the local restaurant attended, and he explained he had a son with spina bifida and would like to meet Tiana.

Explain what happened to Tiana.

Tiana and the teacher went to lunch at the local restaurant and met the manager. Using a few words and her communication device, Tiana communicated that she wanted to work in the kitchen. The kitchen was very small, but the manager felt confident he could make it work. Tiana was hired 3 days a week to weigh and package food prep items. Several adaptations were made given Tiana's physical and visual disabilities. First, a small fan was attached to the back of her wheelchair to blow open the plastic bags for the food. The plastic bags were attached to a large metal bookend and bent at an angle so the fan would blow open the bag when Tiana used her fist to loosen the top of the bag. A small digital scale was also put on her tray, and Tiana, using her "good hand," would place the food items until the scale beeped to indicate 3 ounces. Tiana took the cardboard container and dumped the food into the bag, then took her fist and pulled the full bag off, dropping it into a large container filled with ice sitting next to her wheelchair. Every 30 minutes, one of the kitchen staff gathered the bags and brought them to the cooler. Her goal was to complete 50 to 60 bags in the 2 hours she worked.

CASE STUDY: HAS NO SKILLS—NOT PREPARED TO WORK Rajish is a young man with autism and is nonverbal—when asked where he wanted to work, he would point to his teacher's shirt and tie. It was not clear what Rajish wanted to do. Since Rajish has no verbal means of communication, teachers were unsure what about wearing a shirt and tie appealed to him. Teachers needed more information in order to better understand and interpret what Rajish's gestures meant. Rajish's teachers tried words, pictures, and his communication device to try and understand the appeal and interest of wearing a tie that Rajish seemed to be pointing to.

What questions can you ask?

- What is the purpose of education for any student? To compete in a global economy? To prepare workers for the 21st century? To create lifelong learners? To develop citizens who can contribute to their communities? Why would it not be the same for a student with a disability?
- What is Rajish trying to communicate to us?
- What are Rajish's skills and interests?

How can this situation be reframed?

Brainstorm job possibilities in the downtown area, and then take Rajish to various business and see where he gravitates to. Talk to the family and find out if there is a connection in an office for Rajish.

What else would you do?

The teacher walked around downtown with Rajish and went into various office buildings to identify what his interest was. Rajish wore a shirt and tie and would walk into the offices where people were "dressed up" with a big smile. The teacher looked to see what types of business were located in each of the buildings they visited. One building included a large insurance company that had offices on multiple floors.

Explain what happened to Rajish.

The teacher conducted an informational interview with several of the businesses located in the office buildings. After the teacher's informational interview with the large insurance company, the HR manager suggested Rajish come in to tour the mailroom. The mailroom not only distributed mail to all the different floors but also delivered files for to various staff throughout the firm. Rajish completed a summer internship with the support of a local adult services agency, and the company hired him to work part time once his internship ended. Initially, his parents did not want Rajish to work because they thought it would jeopardize his Supplemental Security Income (SSI) benefits. The teacher worked with the family, and a benefits analysis was completed by the local benefits specialist. Once the parents realized that his working part time was actually beneficial financially, they agreed to allow Rajish to work. His duties have since been expanded to scanning insurance files and creating files for new business on the company cloud.

CASE STUDY: INAPPROPRIATE BEHAVIOR Jeremy uses inappropriate language (profanity). For the past 2 years, he has been on a behavior plan to decrease the use of this language but with no significant change. Because of the lack of improvement, Jeremy was not considered for employment, as it was felt his communication would be too offensive for any workplace. The decision was made that Jeremy must demonstrate no profanity while in school before efforts to find him a job would be made.

What questions can you ask?

- Why does Jeremy use this type of language? Does he get reinforced inadvertently?
- What is the root cause of Jeremy's profanity use? Was a functional behavioral analysis completed to determine when, why, and how often he uses profanity?
- Is the behavior plan appropriate? Is it implemented consistently by all who interact with Jeremy?

How can this situation be reframed?

Instead of stopping a behavior, determine if it is possible to curb the behavior or replace it with something else (e.g., find new words he can use instead). Another option is to brainstorm positions in businesses where using inappropriate language may not be an issue.

What else would you do?

The teacher spent time getting to know Jeremy outside of school. She visited his home and observed him in different situations at school, paying close attention to his use of profanity. Interestingly, the teacher noticed that the students Jeremy emulated also used profanity, but unlike Jeremy, they understood the rules of when and where it was appropriate. While at home, it was discovered that the family did not do anything to reduce his swearing; as with all the other issues, they had to pick and choose their battles.

Explain what happened to Jeremy.

The teacher met with a trucking logistics company. During the tour, she heard a lot of swearing. When asked, the manager said that this happens a lot. The teacher talked about Jeremy and his skills and explained that he would fit into the work culture given his use of profanity. The manager agreed to an internship, and Jeremy was hired part time to assist the drivers in loading their trucks.

CASE STUDY: PARENTS DO NOT WANT THEM TO WORK—THEY CHOOSE NOT TO WORK   Tyree was eager to go to work and talked about it frequently at school. He told everyone he wanted to work with cars. As Tyree was close to graduating from school, his teacher began connecting him with vocational rehabilitation and the local service provider who could help him with employment. When the adult services personnel met with Tyree and his dad, they were surprised to hear that neither one of them was interested in Tyree becoming employed once he left school. In fact, both of them said that Tyree wasn't going to work and that he had no plans to do anything once he left school.

What questions can you ask?

- Why do Tyree and his dad not want Tyree to work?
- Does Tyree understand what work means?
- Are benefits or other factors influencing dad's decision?
- What does Tyree like to do?
- What are their goals for Tyree?

How can this situation be reframed?

Visit with Tyree and his dad to find out what concerns they have about Tyree working. Connect Tyree and his dad with other families whose son or daughter has gone to work to share their experiences. Then, arrange opportunities for Tyree to explore a variety of businesses and see what interests him.

What else would you do?

The teacher called a team meeting with Tyree and his dad. During the discussion, it was revealed that Tyree's dad was a mechanic who had sustained a hand injury and was unable to work. He and Tyree had become good buddies and hung out together. Since Tyree's mom had died, Tyree and his dad were very close. Dad wanted Tyree to follow in his footsteps but knew Tyree could not become a mechanic.

Explain what happened to Tyler.

Tyree's dad became an asset to the job development process. Through his connections, businesses in the community related to mechanical work were brainstormed. The teacher followed up with the contacts. Tyree visited several companies, such as an auto parts store, gas stations, department stores with an auto section, car washes, and new car dealerships. An internship was arranged in the parts department of a car dealership. Tyree was responsible for stocking and straightening shelves and pulling parts for the mechanics and customers. It was arranged for his dad to drive Tyree to and from work, giving him "tips" along the way. The company was so impressed that they hired Tyree part time as an auto parts assistant. Now Tyree and his dad hang out and "talk shop" together on weekends and after work hours.

CASE STUDY: SMALL TOWN/RURAL AREA   Michael has an intellectual disability and lives in a small rural community. The town has a population of 2,000 and a small downtown area with a few shops, a gas station, a medical office, a veterinary clinic, a fast-food and sit-down restaurant, town hall, a law office, a sheriff's department, a hair salon, and a school.

What questions can you ask?

- Where do other people who live in this small town work?
- What are Michael's skills and interests?
- Why are job development strategies not working?
- What supports would help Michael be successful?

How can this situation be reframed?

Conduct a labor market analysis in the community by researching future growth plans, local labor market needs, and what the economy can support. Explore business options in nearby cities if accessible. Can a satellite be developed in the community? Can it be replicated as a self-employment option? Can a job be found and carpooling be arranged with another member of the community who works there?

Develop business relationships and promote the talents of your students. Word of mouth and relationships are key strategies for finding jobs in any community and even more so in a small town where everyone knows everyone.

Explain what happened to Michael.

The teacher spent time visiting businesses and getting to know the hiring people at local events that were held in the community. She found opportunities to create situations presenting her students as competent workers. For example, she conducted onsite situational assessments, shared success stories, and connected new businesses with previous employers who served as references to dispel misconceptions resulting from the unsuccessful past experiences of several businesses that had hired adults with disabilities who did not have the necessary supports. She began looking at what would be a benefit for her students and, with the support of her administration, created a school-based bakery that her students could run side by side with students without disabilities. The bakery was opened to the community and filled a need for fresh-baked goods. Students got to know the customers and built their résumé while gaining valuable skills. The teacher began arranging to conduct 4-hour situational assessments and internships in a variety of businesses, turning some work experiences into permanent jobs. Through these opportunities, she was able to get a good idea of what Michael liked to do and the environments he thrived best in. Michael liked to push buttons, listen to water, and fold—a perfect match for a laundry position. The few jobs available in the community that matched Michael's qualities were already taken, but a fitness gym was soon to be opened, and the idea of a laundry service arose. With the help of vocational rehabilitation, Michael became a small-business owner himself, installing an industrial-sized washer and dryer in his home. The hair salon and fitness center contracted with Michael's laundry service to pick up their soiled towels; wash, sterilize, and fold them; and return a batch of clean towels the next morning. Word of mouth became his primary marketing tool, and before long, Michael had four other businesses to add to his list of customers.

CASE STUDY: THERE ARE NO JOBS AVAILABLE   Employers are always hiring! Even during times of recession, tasks need to get done.

What job-specific questions can you ask?

- When is your busy season?
- Do you offer seasonal work?
- What benefits do you offer for part-time employees?
- Do any of your employees work flexible schedules?
- Do any of your employees split shifts?
- Do people get together after work?

What employer-specific questions can you ask?

- Can you explain your business's product (or service) in more detail?
- What is the structure of your organization?
- What do you like most about working here?
- What are your areas of highest turnover?
- Do you have written job descriptions?
- What expectations do you have of your employees?
- What do you value most in your employees?

How can this situation be reframed?

Broaden your perspective. Instead of sitting back determining what your students can do, get out in the business community and find out what kinds of jobs are available and match your students to the real possibilities. Involve employers in your education programs, and remember that you are preparing the next-generation workforce for these employers and they would greatly appreciate having you prepare workers with the skills and attributes that will meet their needs. Develop business relationships by visiting local businesses, arranging work experiences and internships for your students, making connections so you know when a job opening comes up, and networking with other employment services to share job leads.

What else would you do?

Invite employers to come talk with your students. Create a culture of employment in the classroom.

Explain what happened.

The teacher created presentations for his local school board meetings and encouraged each school board member to identify one business (theirs or another) to refer to him. The teacher then presented at local chamber of commerce, Rotary club, and small business group lunches and brought a student and an employer along to tell their story.

CHALLENGES THAT TEACHERS FACE

Broader than these and other challenging individual situations connected to individual students, the effort to promote effective postschool employment outcomes for our students also requires teachers to face more generalized challenges.

Challenge 1: Ours Is a Big Job

Not the least of the more systemic challenges is that promoting postschool employment for students with disabilities is a big and complex job. Transition crosses educational and service agency boundaries; it confronts social and cultural norms and stereotypical thinking; it addresses perceptions students have of themselves. It requires creating opportunities for students to safely and systematically explore the world of work in ways that afford them the opportunity to develop and practice important communication skills. This diversity of issues is daunting. It is hard for one person alone to do this job and to gain and keep any kind of momentum.

What to Do? Finding a real collaborator in an outside organization or agency who is at least as passionate about the students and issues as you are is helpful. It is important to find someone who can create a new vision and share the workload. Two heads (or a couple more) are better than one here. Combining experiences, talents, and ideas will yield a product and a process that is greater than any one person could accomplish alone. Having at least one other person in the mix also allows you to hold each other accountable for getting things planned and done. Together, you can tackle the stumbling blocks *and* celebrate and promote successes.

Challenge 2: Learned Passivity

One of the surprising things teachers and other educational/adult services professionals are likely to encounter when they begin engaging students in this more participatory approach to teaching is a kind of learning that many students demonstrate in response. That is, the student's experience has often been that not much actual classroom participation is expected of them and that simply by functioning "on cruise control," they can get through the day, the week, and maybe the year. They are reluctant to participate.

What to Do? Help students identify their own style of learning. Use one of the learning style assessment models to help students get a new and practical sense of themselves as learners. Legitimize their style. Demonstrate to them where their style of learning is useful and where it may work to their disadvantage. Encourage them to expand on their style of learning. Then, set high expectations. Explain that employability is a subject that is about their immediate future. Indicate that this is a fairly risk-free opportunity to explore the world of work that will pay dividends directly to them. *Expect* them to reach beyond their comfort level—and guide and support them along the way. Finally, give them a very concrete set of lessons to follow and help them recognize how the particular lessons are important to their success and how they build on one another to achieve that success.

Challenge 3: Self-Doubt

Many educational and counseling professionals assume that the primary need of students with disabilities is to learn self-determination skills. They do need to become more self-determined, but first they need to see themselves as actually having the capacity to learn. That is, they need to have a genuine sense of self-efficacy. They need to demonstrate to themselves first (and later, to others) that they can perform the tasks they are asked to perform at the level of competency they need to succeed.

What to Do? A significant part of building a student's self-efficacy can be achieved by always operating from a strengths-based perspective in the classroom. Just as students should learn what their personal learning styles are, they should also learn what their strengths are. This can be done using things like the assessments and tools offered through packages such as Tom Rath's StrengthsFinder (Rath, 2007). (See also Positive Personal Profile discussed in Chapter 3.) Strengths-based content, language, and feedback students receive should be part of the everyday classroom routine. Further, the teaching strategy of modeling your own thinking while performing a task—including the stops, starts, mistakes, and successes—profoundly demonstrates the realities of human thinking and learning while improving a student's own thinking skills. Another valuable teaching strategy, when used at appropriate times, involves exploring (orally or in writing) three ways a situation could have gone better, three ways it could have gone worse, and three alternatives to the way it was handled. Imagine aloud what someone whom you greatly respect would have done, or think about what advice you would give to someone facing a similar situation.

Challenge 4: Momentum

Even with a small but passionate team of collaborators, it is hard to keep and sustain momentum in this work. So, some quick rules of thumb are helpful:

1. Keep your eye on the prize. This is truly a worthy and admirable goal. Even what we might consider to be small successes are life changing for your students.

2. Set one or two powerful goals. That is, set a couple of goals that, once accomplished, will help your efforts get some notice by others and hopefully gain their support.

3. Get organized. After setting your goals, decide what steps make sense for your team to take to accomplish those goals. Decide who is going to do what—and when—to make things happen. Create a time line and work to stick to it, making purposeful modifications when needed.

4. Celebrate your successes—big and small—together!

PULLING IT ALL TOGETHER

This book has outlined proven strategies developed by educators, transition coordinators, and adult services personnel that result in postschool employment outcomes for students with disabilities. It is not uncommon for all of us to receive a lot of good information and resources that would be useful for transition-age youth. However, when we get caught up in our day-to-day activities, it can feel too overwhelming to implement them. Transition plans are developed to help organize this process for students. The Implementing Transition Action Plan (ITAP) is introduced to organize the process for professionals (Figure 7.1). This tool, developed by and for the professionals responsible for transition services, can be a useful guide to help plan, individualize, and implement the process and techniques described in this book. Each component of the ITAP corresponds to the representative chapter and highlights the key points to assist with thinking through how to move forward and, most important, how to put the content into action.

The ITAP will keep the key components of supporting students in their transition from school to work organized and provide you with the structure to ensure each area is addressed. To use this tool, identify which area you are focusing on now (some areas may take longer than others, and some areas, such as assessment, are ongoing). For example, if you are working with an eighth-grade student, you may begin with planning for employment as the area of focus. Identify your current status (what are you doing to help students plan for employment?) and your vision (what would you like to see for your students?). From there, write down what you would like to accomplish with your students (goals) and the steps necessary to get there (action steps), along with who you will need to collaborate with (think of all the organizations and people you will need to ensure you meet your goal). Finally, be proactive—what challenges might arise, and what can you do to overcome those challenges? Keep the ITAP on your desk where you can refer back to it each week or month to determine where you are with your plan and what you need to do to continue or change to meet your goal. Examples of considerations important for employment are located in Figure 7.1.

ITAP: Implementing Transition Action Plan

Area of Focus: Employment

Current Status (What are we doing in this area?):

- Skills to Pay the Bills sessions in collaboration with adult services provider
- In-school volunteer work—school office, school engineer
- Beginning transition portfolios for all students

Vision (What would I like to see?):

- All students have a transition portfolio that includes Positive Personal Profile (PPP), visual résumé, letters of reference for internships, evaluations from internships
- All students participate in internships based on their interests in various businesses (one per semester)
- Develop a service-based learning with Habitat for Humanity
- Create a school-led enterprise (e.g., coffee shop, snack bar, supply store)

Goals (What do I want to accomplish?):

- Complete positive personal profiles with all students
- Research school-led enterprises with class and identify the best option
- Develop internships with four to five local businesses based on student interests
- Conduct annual transition fair

Collaboration (Who do I need to bring together to make sure these tasks get done?):

- SCORE (https://www.score.org)
- Vocational rehabilitation
- Adult services agencies
- Business teacher
- Parent liaison

Action Steps (What do I need to do?):

- Contact SCORE for possible mentor
- Contact vocational rehabilitation and adult services agencies to develop a committee for transition fair
- Work with business teacher and local organizations to identify internship possibilities
- Work with parent liaison to help with transition fair and contact parents

Strategies (What issues might I encounter, and how can I address them?):

- People are too busy to meet—consider video conference calls
- Time to complete the PPPs—develop a timeline and divide students out to complete two per week
- Funding for setting up school-based enterprise or transportation to and from internship sites
    - Contact local foundations or business groups (Lions, Rotary, small business associations) and identify mini grant opportunities
    - Collaborate with business teacher to identify transportation used for school work experiences
    - Look at different scheduling options (e.g., students go straight to their internship in the morning with transportation needed only one way back to school); identify internships closer to school within walking distance
    - Collaborate with adult services providers and vocational rehabilitation for transportation

Figure 7.1. Implementing Transition Action Plan (ITAP).

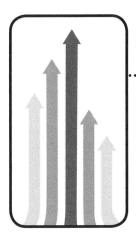

References

CHAPTER 1

Association of People Supporting Employment First (APSE). (n.d.). Retrieved from http://www.apse.org

Bureau of Labor Statistics, U.S. Department of Labor. (2019, February 26). Persons with a disability: Labor force characteristics–2018 [Press release]. Retrieved from https://www.bls.gov/news.release/pdf/disabl.pdf

Disabled World (2016). Disability Facts Statistics Retrieved from https://www.disabled-world.com/disability/statistics-2/

Fessler, P. (Producer). (2015, July 23). Why disability and poverty still go hand in hand 25 years after landmark law [Radio broadcast episode]. https://www.npr.org/sections/health-shots/2015/07/23/424990474/why-disability-and-poverty-still-go-hand-in-hand-25-years-after-landmark-law

National Association of State Directors of Developmental Disabilities Services & Human Services Research Institute, (2018).

National Core Indicator Data Brief (September, 2018). Retrieved from https://www.nationalcoreindicators.org/upload/core-indicators/NCIEmployment_Update3_DataBrief.pdf

National Association of Workforce Boards. (n.d.). Retrieved from https://www.nawb.org/wioa_resources.asp

National Council on Disability. (2017). *National disability policy: A progress report–October 2017.* Washington, DC: National Council on Disability.

National Center on Leadership for the Employment and Economic Advancement of People with Disabilities (2014). Summary of major policies included in Titles I and IV of the Workforce Innovations and Opportunity Act. Retrieved from http://wwwleadcenter.org/system/files/resource/downloadable_version/WIOA_Policy_Brief_10.22.14.pdf.

Newman, L., Wagner, M., Knokey, A.-M., Marder, C., Nagle, K., Shaver, D., Wei, X., with Cameto, R., Contreras, E., Ferguson, K., Greene, S., & Schwarting, M. (2011). *The post-high school outcomes of young adults with disabilities up to 8 years after high school. A report from the National Longitudinal Transition Study-2 (NLTS2)* (NCSER 2011-3005). Menlo Park, CA: SRI International. Retrieved from www.nlts2.org/reports

Office of Disability Employment Policy. (n.d.). New resource on WIOA from a disability perspective. Lead Center. Retrieved from http://www.leadcenter.org/news/newsletters/lead-december-2014

Office of Disability Employment Policy. (n.d.). Retrieved from https://www.dol.gov/odep/topics/EmploymentFirst.htm

Parent-Johnson, W., & Parent-Johnson, R. (2015, May). *Transition from pediatric to adult medical care for youth with disabilities and/or chronic health conditions.* Presentation, 2015 IASSID (International Association of the Scientific Study of Intellectual & Developmental Disabilities) Americas, Regional Congress, Honolulu, HI.

Portes, A. (1998). Social capital: Its origins and applications in modern sociology. *Annual Review of Sociology, 24*(1), 1–24. https://doi.org/10/1146/annurev.soc.24.1.1

Siperstein, G. N., Heyman, M., & Stokes, J. E. (2014). Pathways to employment: A national survey of adults with intellectual disabilities. *Journal of Vocational Rehabilitation, 41*(3), 165–178. https://doi.org/10.3233/JVR-140711

Test, D. W., Mazzotti, V. L., Mustain, A. L., Kortering, L., & Kohler. P. (2009). Evidence-based secondary transition predictors for improving postschool outcomes for students with disabilities. *Career Development for Exceptional Individuals, 32*(3), 160–181. https://doi.org/10.1177/0885728809346960

U.S. Census Bureau. (2016). 2017 U.S. Census bureau disability statistics facts for features. Retrieved from https://www.disabled-world.com/disability/statistics/cbfff.php

U.S. Department of Labor. (2016). Office of Disability Employment Policy. Retrieved from https://www.dol.gov/odep

Vallas, R., & Fremstad, S. (2014). A simple but critical fix is needed now for the nation's disability system. *The Atlantic.* Retrieved from https://www.theatlantic.com/politics/archive/2014/09/a-simple-but-critical-fix-is-needed-now-for-the-nations-disability-system/431301

Wehman, P. (2013). Transition from school to work: Where are we and where do we need to go? *Career Development and Transition for Exceptional Individuals, 36*(1), 58–66. https://doi.org/10.1177%2F2165143413482137

World Health Organization. (2011). World report on disability. Retrieved from https://www.who.int/disabilities/world_report/2011/report.pdf

CHAPTER 2

Antosh, A. A., & Association of University Centers on Disabilities. (2013, April). *A collaborative interagency, interdisciplinary approach to transition from adolescence to adulthood.* Silver Spring, MD: Association of University Centers on Disabilities.

Arnett, J. J. (2000). Emerging adulthood: A theory of development from the late teens through the twenties. *American Psychologist, 55*(5), 469–480. https://doi.org/10.1037//0003-066X.55.5.469

Assistive Technology Act of 1998, Pub.L. No. 105-394, 112 STAT. 3627 (1998).

Bandura, A. (1997). *Self-efficacy: The exercise of control.* New York: W.H. Freeman.

Cobb, R. B., & Alwell, M. (2009). Transition planning/coordinating interventions for youth with disabilities: A systematic review. *Career Development for Exceptional Individuals, 32*(2), 70–81. https://doi.org/10.1177/0885728809336655

Felder, R. M., & Silverman, L. K. (2002). Learning and teaching styles in engineering education. *Engineering Education, 78*(7), 674–681.

Individuals with Disabilities Education Improvement Act, 20 U.S.C. 1411[d] § 300.704 (2004).

Kania, J., & Kramer, M. (2011, Winter). Stanford social innovation review: Collective impact. *Stanford Social Innovation Review.* Retrieved from https://ssir.org/articles/entry/collective_impact

Kline, F. M., Schumaker, J. B., & Deshler, D. D. (1991). Development and validation of feedback routines for instructing students with learning disabilities. *Learning Disability Quarterly, 14*(3), 191–207. https://doi.org/10.2307/1510849

Kolb, A. Y., & Kolb, D. A. (2005). Learning styles and learning spaces: Enhancing experiential learning in higher education. *Academy of Management Learning & Education, 4*(2), 193–212. https://doi.org/10.5465/amle.2005.17268566

Lancaster, P., & Johnson, D. R. (2005). *Road to success.* Lawrence: University of Kansas.

Landmark, L. J., Ju, S., & Zhang, D. (2010). Substantiated best practices in transition: Fifteen plus years later. *Career Development for Exceptional Individuals, 33*(3), 165–176. https://doi.org/10.1177/0885728810376410

Mithaug, D. E. (1993). *Self-regulation theory: How optimal adjustment maximizes gain.* Westport, CT: Praeger.

Mithaug, D. E. (1996). *Equal opportunity theory.* Thousand Oaks, CA: Sage.

Mithaug, D. E., Agran, M. Martin, M., & Wehmeyer, M. L. (2003). *Self-determined learning theory: Construction, verification, and evaluation.* Mahwah, NJ: Erlbaum.

National Collaborative on Workforce and Disability (NCWD, 2018). Retrieved from http://www.ncwd-youth.info

Noonan, P. M., Erickson, A. G., & Morningstar, M. E. (2012). Effects of community transition teams on interagency collaboration for schools and adult agency staff. *Career Development and Transition for Exceptional Individuals, 36*(2), 96–104. doi: https://doi.org/10.1177/2165143412451119

Pajares, F., & Urdan, T. C. (2006). Self-efficacy beliefs of adolescents. Greenwich, CT: Information Age.

Palincsar, A. S., Magnusson, S. J., Cutter, J., & Vincent, M. (2002). Supporting guided-inquiry instruction. *Council for Exceptional Children, 34*(3), 88.

Tett, G. (2015). *The silo effect: The peril of expertise and the promise of breaking down barriers.* New York, NY: Simon & Schuster.

Wehmeyer, M. L. (1996). Self-determination as an educational outcome: Why is it important to children, youth, and adults with disabilities? In D. J. Sands & M. L. Wehmeyer (Eds.), *Self-determination across the lifespan: Independence and choices for people with disabilities* (pp. 17–35). Baltimore, MD: Paul H. Brookes Publishing Co.

Wehmeyer, M. L. (1997). Self-determination as an education outcome: A definitional framework and implications for intervention. *Journal of Developmental and Physical Disabilities, 9*(3), 175–209. https://doi.org/10.1023/A:1024981820074

Wehmeyer, M. L. (1999). A functional model of self-determination. *Focus on Autism and Other Developmental Disabilities, 14*(1), 53–61. https://doi.org/10.1177/108835769901400107

Wehmeyer, M. L. (2006). Universal design for learning, access to the general education curriculum and students with mild mental retardation. *Exceptionality, 14*(4), 225–235. https://doi.org/10.1207/s15327035ex1404_4

Wehmeyer, M. L., Yeager, D., Bolding, N., Agran, M., & Hughes, C. (2003). The effects of self-regulation strategies on goal attainment for students with developmental disabilities in general education classroom. *Journal of Developmental and Physical Disabilities, 15*(1), 79–91. https://doi.org/10.1023/A:1021408405270

CHAPTER 3

Benz, M. R., Lindstrom, L., & Yovanoff, P. (2000). Improving graduation and employment outcomes of students with disabilities: Predictive factors and student perspectives. *Exceptional Children, 66*(4), 509–529. https://doi.org/10.1177/001440290006600405

Carter, E. W., Austin, D., & Trainor, A. A. (2012). Predictors of postschool employment outcomes for young adults with severe disabilities. *Journal of Disability Policy Studies,23*(1), 50–63. https://doi.org/10.1177/1044207311414680

Carter, E. W., Trainor, A. A., Cakiroglu, O., Swedeen, B., & Owens, L. A. (2010). Availability of and access to career development activities for transition-age youth with disabilities. *Career Development for Exceptional Individuals, 33*(1), 13–24. https://doi.org/10.1177/0885728809344332

U.S. Department of Labor (n.d.) Self-Employment & Entrepreneurship. Retrieved from https://www.dol.gov/odep/topics/SelfEmploymentEntrepreneurship.htm

Forest, M., & Lusthaus, E. (1990). Everyone belongs with MAPS action planning system. *Teaching Exceptional Children, 22*(2), 32–35. https://doi.org/10.1177/004005999002200210

Forest, M. & Pearpoint, J. Common sense tools: MAPS and CIRCLES for inclusive education. (n.d.). Retrieved from http://www.inclusion.com/artcommonsensetools.html

Hagner, D., Helm, D., & Butterworth, J. (1996). "This is your meeting": A qualitative study of person-centered planning. *Mental Retardation, 34*(3), 159–171.

Joe, P. (n.d.). Poppin Joe's™ Gourmet Kettle Korn | Welcome. Retrieved from http://poppinjoes.org

Kincaid, D., Knab, J. T., & Clark, H. B. (2005). Person-centered planning. In M. Hersen & J. Rosqvist (Eds.), *Encyclopedia of behavior modification and cognitive behavior therapy* (pp. 429–431). Thousand Oaks, CA: Sage.

Niemiec, B., Lavin, D., & Owens, L. A. (2009). Establishing a national employment first agenda. *Journal of Vocational Rehabilitation, 31*(3), 139–144. https://doi.org/10.3233/JVR-2009-0483

O'Brien, J., & Lovett, H. (1993). *Finding a way toward everyday lives: The contribution of person centered planning.* Harrisburg: Pennsylvania Office of Mental Retardation.

Pearpoint, J., Forest, M., & O'Brien, J. (1993). *PATH: A workbook for planning positive possible futures: Planning alternative tomorrows with hope for schools, organizations, businesses, families.* Toronto, Ont.: Inclusion Press.

Social Security Administration. (2018). *2018 Red Book.* Retrieved from https://www.ssa.gov/redbook

Smull, M., Sanderson, H., & Allen, B. (2001). *Essential lifestyle planning: A handbook for facilitators.* Manchester, UK: North West Training and Development Team.

Test, D. W., Mazzotti, V. L., Mustain, A. L., Kortering, L., & Kohler, P. (2009). Evidence-based secondary transition predictors for improving postschool outcomes for students with disabilities. *Career Development for Exceptional Individuals, 32*(3), 160–181. https://doi.org/10.1177/0885728809346960

Turnbull, A., & Turnbull, R. (1992). Group action planning (GAP). *Families and Disability Newsletter,* 1–13.

WINTAC (2018). Retrieved from http://www.wintac.org/

Zemeckis, R. (Director). (1994). *Forrest Gump* [Motion picture]. United States: Paramount Pictures.

CHAPTER 4

Future, Inc. (n.d.). Explore careers. Retrieved from https://mappingyourfuture.org/planyourcareer

Nazarov, Z. E., Golden, T. P., & von Schrader, S. (2012). Prevocational services and supported employment wages. *Journal of Vocational Rehabilitation, 37*(2), 119–129. https://doi.org/10.3233/JVR-2012-0605

National Technical Assistance Center on Transition. (2011). Retrieved from https://transitionta.org/

Office of Special Education and Rehabilitative Services United States Department of Education. (2017). *A transition guide to postsecondary education and employment for students and youth with disabilities.* Washington, DC: U.S. Department of Education.

Parent-Johnson, W., & Tanis, S. (2014, December). SD Futures curriculum: Achieving self-directed employment through a web-based curriculum. Sioux Falls, SD: Authors. Final report submitted to the U.S. Department of Education, Office of Special Education and Rehabilitative Services Programs.

SD Division of Rehabilitation Services, 2018. Forms & publications. (2018). Retrieved from http://dhs.sd.gov/rehabservices/default.aspx

Simonsen, M., Fabian, E., & Luecking, R. (2015). Employer preferences in hiring youth with disabilities. *Journal of Rehabilitation, 81*(1), 9–18. Retrieved from https://www.researchgate.net/publication/279325601_Employer_Preferences_in_Hiring_Youth_with_Disabilities

Test, D. W., Mazzotti, V. L., Mustain, A. L., Kortering, L., & Kohler. P. (2009). Evidence-based secondary transition predictors for improving postschool outcomes for students with disabilities. *Career Development for Exceptional Individuals, 32*(3), 160–181. https://doi.org/10.1177/0885728809346960

Wehman, P. (2009). Editorial. *Journal of Vocational Rehabilitation, 31*(3), 137–138. https://doi.org/10.3233/JVR-2009-0482

Wehman, P. (2011). *Essentials of transition planning.* Baltimore, MD: Paul H. Brookes Publishing Co.

Zickuhr, K., & Smith, A. (2012). Digital differences. Pew Research Center Internet and Technology. Retrieved from http://www.pewinternet.org/2012/04/13/digital-differences

CHAPTER 5

Allison, R., Hyatt, J., Owens, L., Clark, K. A., & Test, D. W. (2017). Competitive integrated employment toolkit. National Technical Assistance Center on Transition. Retrieved from https://transitionta.org/cietoolkit

Benz, M. R., Lindstrom, L., & Yovanoff, P. (2000). Improving graduation and employment outcomes of students with disabilities: Predictive factors and student perspectives. *Exceptional Children, 66*(4), 509–529. https://doi.org/10.1177/001440290006600405

Carter, E. W., Austin, D., & Trainor, A. A. (2012). Predictors of postschool employment outcomes for young adults with severe disabilities. *Journal of Disability Policy Studies, 23*(1), 50–63. https://doi.org/10.1177/1044207311414680

Test, D. W., Mazzotti, V. L., Mustian, A. L., Fowler, C. H., Kortering, L., & Kohler, P. (2009). Evidence-based secondary transition predictors for improving postschool outcomes for students with disabilities. *Career Development for Exceptional Individuals, 32*(3), 160–181. https://doi.org/10.1177/0885728809346960

Workforce Innovation and Opportunity Act (PL 113-128) (2014).

CHAPTER 6

Daston, M., Riehle, J. E., & Rutkowski, S. (2012). *High school transition that works: Lessons learned from Project SEARCH.* Baltimore, MD: Paul H. Brookes Publishing Co.

Gold, M. (1978). *Try another way: Training manual.* Austin, TX: Marc Gold & Associates.

Hughes, C., & Carter, E. W. (2012). *The new transition handbook: Strategies high school teachers use that work!* Baltimore, MD: Paul H. Brookes Publishing Co.

Shogren, K. A. (2013). A social–ecological analysis of the self-determination literature. *Intellectual and Developmental Disabilities, 51*(6), 496–511. https://doi.org/10.1352/1934-9556-51.6.496

Snell, M. E., & Brown, F. E. (2006). *Instruction of students with severe disabilities* (6th ed.). New York, NY: Pearson.

Storey, K., & Miner, C. A. (2011). *Systematic instruction of functional skills for students and adults with disabilities.* Springfield, IL: Charles C. Thomas.

Wehmeyer, M., & Parent, W. (2011). *Research to practice in self-determination series. National Gateway to Self-Determination.* Kansas City, MO: Institute for Human Development.

Wehmeyer, M. L., Parent, W., Lattimore, J., Obremski, S., Poston, D., & Rousso, H. (2009). Promoting self-determination and self-directed employment planning for young women with disabilities. *Journal of Social Work in Disability & Rehabilitation,* 8(3–4), 117–131. https://doi.org/10.1080/15367100903200429

CHAPTER 7

Crawford, L. E., & Cacioppo, J. T. (2002). Learning where to look for danger: Integrating affective and spatial information. *Psychological Science, 13*(5), 449–453. https://doi.org/10.1111/1467-9280.00479

Force, N. (2018, July 8). Humor, neuroplasticity and the power to change your mind [Web log post]. Retrieved from https://psychcentral.com/blog/humor-neuroplasticity-and-the-power-to-change-your-mind

Rath, T. (2007). *StrengthsFinder 2.0.* New York, NY: Gallup Press.

Rozin, P., & Royzman, E. B. (2001). Negativity bias, negativity dominance, and contagion. *Personality and Social Psychology Review, 5*(4), 296–320. https://doi.org/10.1207/s15327957pspr0504_2

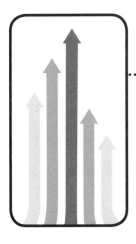

Index

Note: Page numbers followed by *f*, *b*, and *t* indicate figures, boxes, and tables, respectively.

ADA, *see* Americans with Disabilities Act of 1990
Adult services agencies, 42–43, 63–65, 89
Americans with Disabilities Act (ADA) of 1990
    (PL 101-336), 3, 42
Application and interview process, 80
Assistive technology, 98

Barriers to employment, severe disability as, 112–113
Benefits planning, 42
Best practices, 17–25
    collective impact at the organizational level, 23
    common agenda, 24
    developing and/or using universally designed methods
        and materials, 22
    elaborated feedback, 19–20
    establishing a shared measurement system, 24
    learning as social and guided activity, 21, 22*b*
    learning how you and your students learn, 20–21
    maintaining continuous communication, 25
    modeling, 18
    participating in mutually reinforcing activities, 24–25
    role playing by students, 18–19
Bias, negative, 107–108
Business community, knowing the, 68–69
Business knowledge, 69–70
Business partnership agreement, internship, 81

Career and technical education programs, 62
Career exploration tools, 54
Centers for Medicare & Medicaid Services (CMS), 3
Charting my own course, 12
Churchill, W., 108
CMS, *see* Centers for Medicare & Medicaid Services
Collaboration, importance of, 8–10
Collective impact
    growing your own team for, 10
    at the organizational level, 23
    practical application of, 11–17
Common agenda, 11, 13, 24

Common Core State Standards, 43
Communication, continuous, 25
Community work incentive coordinator (CWIC), 42
Community work opportunities, 61–63, 111
    reframing a perceived lack of, 116–117
    in small towns/rural areas, 115–116
Compensatory strategies, 100
Competitive integrated employment, 67–68
Consumer situational assessment form, 55–59
Contacts, maintaining a database of, 77
Continuous communication, 25
Counselors and adult service professionals, 15
Curriculum development, 11
    Common Core State Standards and, 43
    comprehensive sets of lessons or topics in, 12–17
CWIC, *see* community work incentive coordinator

Deciding on employment options, 43–46
Desire to work, 114–115
Destination, getting to my, 13
Developing and/or using universally designed methods
    and materials, 22
Development of high school services, 48–51
Disabled persons, *see* persons with disabilities
Discovering my own path, 12

Education of All Handicapped Children Act of 1975
    (PL 94-142), 2
Elaborated feedback, 19–20
Employee progress report, 64*f*
Employers
    application and interview process of, 80
    business knowledge and, 69–70
    competitive integrated employment and, 67–68
    developing employment proposals for, 77, 78*f*
    evaluation process and, 83
    informational interviews with, 74, 75*f*–76*f*, 80
    intern criteria and job descriptions for, 80
    knowing the business community and, 68–69

Employers–*continued*
  meeting with, 74–77
  negotiations with, 101
  networking with, 70–71, 72–73*f*
  partnership agreements with, 80
  preparing students for, through work-based learning
    or internships, 77–79
  worksite analysis with, 80, 82*f*
Employment First, 33–34, 68
Employment of persons with disabilities
  changing the landscape of disability and, 3–5
  deciding on options for, 43–46
  importance of, 2
  preparing students for, 77–79
  probationary period in, 30–31
  self-, 45
  in small towns/rural areas, 115–116
  statistics on, 2–3
  see also internships; persons with disabilities
Employment proposals, 77, 78*f*
Environmental modifications, 98–100
Evaluation process, 83, 85*f*–88*f*
Exploration of careers, *see* school experience
Exposure to experiences and motivation, 29, 30*f*

FACTS strategy for job interviews, 18, 19*f*
Fading plan, 103*f*, 105
Failure, learning from, 29
Feedback, elaborated, 19–20
Field observations, 15, 16*f*
Fight-or-flight response, 107
Final internship evaluation form, 86*f*–88*f*
Finding the right adult services agency, 42–43
Flexible work schedules, 98–99
Following up and maintaining contacts, 77
Forms
  consumer situational assessment, 55*f*–59*f*
  employee progress report, 64*f*
  employment proposal, 78*f*
  fading plan, 103*f*
  field observation, 16*f*
  final internship evaluation, 85*f*
  informational interview, 75*f*–76*f*
  instructional plans, 96*f*
  internship business partner agreement, 81*f*
  internship performance evaluation, 85*f*
  job observation assessment, 53*f*
  lesson plan, 14*f*
  networking, 72*f*–73*f*
  observation template, 36*f*
  ongoing support plan, 104*f*
  positive personal profile, 39*f*
  questions to ask supported employment providers, 44*f*
  situational assessment observational, 60*f*
  task analysis, 94*f*
  worksite analysis, 82*f*

Getting to my destination, 13
Goals, unrealistic, 110–111

Guided-inquiry model of teaching and learning, 21
Guiding questions, 12–13

Hands-off model, 8, 9*f*
Hidden job market, 71
High school services, development of, 48–51
Hygiene, poor, 109–110

IDEIA, *see* Individuals with Disabilities Education
    Improvement Act 2004
Identifying instructional strategies and supports, 93
Identifying learning styles and preferences, 51–54
IEP, *see* individualized education program
Impairment-Related Work Expense (IRWE), 42
Implementing provisions for job retention, 102, 105
Implementing Transition Action Plan (ITAP), 119, 120*f*
Inappropriate behavior, 113–114
Index of Learning Styles, 20
Individualized education program (IEP), 1, 29, 41
  Employment First and, 33
Individuals with Disabilities Education Improvement Act
    2004 (IDEIA) (PL 101-476), 8
Informational interviews, 74, 75*f*–76*f*, 80
Instructional Plans, 95, 96*f*
Instructional strategies, 93–95
  identifying, 93
Instructional supports, 93–95
Interest areas, establishing, 63–65
Internships, 61–63, 77–79
  business partnership agreement, 81*f*
  criteria and job description for, 80
  evaluation process in, 83, 85*f*–88*f*
  final evaluation, 86*f*–88*f*
  orientation and training for, 83
  partnership agreements, 80, 81*f*
  performance evaluation, 85*f*
Interviews
  informational, 74, 75*f*–76*f*, 80
  job, 18, 80
IRWE, *see* Impairment-Related Work Expense
ITAP, *see* Implementing Transition Action Plan

Job descriptions, 80
Job interviews, 18, 80
Job observation assessment form, 53*f*
Job retention, 102–105
Job shadowing, 52, 53*f*

Kania, John, 9, 10, 23
Knowing the business community, 68–69
Kolb Learning Style Inventory, 20
Kramer, Mark, 9, 10, 23

Lack of job opportunities, reframing of perceived,
  116–117
Learned passivity, 117–118

Learning
    from failure, 29
    as social and guided activity, 21, 22*b*
    styles of, 20–21, 51–54
Learning styles, 20–21, 51–54
Lesson plans, 13–17
    form for, 14*f*
    guiding questions in, 12–13

Mapping Your Future, 54
Meeting with employers, 74–77
Modeling, 18, 102
Modifications, environmental, 98–100
Momentum, 118
Mutually reinforcing activities, 24–25
My Next Move, 54

National Collaborative on Workforce and Disability
        (NCWD), 8
Natural supports, 95–105
    assistive technology, 98
    compensatory strategies, 100
    employer negotiations, 101
    environmental modifications, 98–100
    implementing provisions for job retention, 102, 105
    responding to work-related and social issues, 101–102
NCWD, *see* National Collaborative on Workforce
        and Disability
Negative bias, 107–108
Negotiations, employer, 101
Networking, 70–71, 72*f*–73*f*

Obama, B., 3
Observation template, 36*f*
Observations, job, 52, 53*f*
Ongoing support plan, 104*f*, 105
Online career exploration tools, 54
Open job market, 71
Orientation, job, 83
Overcoming problems, 107–109
    challenges teachers face with, 117–118
    with few jobs available, 116–117
    with inappropriate behavior, 113–114
    with lack of skills and being unprepared to work, 113
    with living in a small town/rural area, 115–116
    with objections from employers, 77
    with parents not wanting student to work or student
        not wanting to work, 114–115
    with poor hygiene, 109–110
    with severe disability and barriers to employment,
        112–113
    with transportation, 111
    with unrealistic goals, 110–111

Parents not wanting student to work, 114–115
Participant-observers, teachers as, 15
Partnership agreements, 80, 81*f*

PASS, *see* Plan for Achieving Self-Support
Passions, identifying, *see* school experience
Passivity, learned, 117–118
PCP, *see* person-centered planning
Performance evaluation, internship, 85*f*
Person-centered planning (PCP), 28*b*, 33, 46
    importance of, 34
    meeting for, 41
    observation template, 36*f*
    perception in, 37
    positive personal profile in, 39*f*
    process of, 34–40
    time line, 35*b*
    utilizing information from, 41–42
Persons with disabilities
    changing the landscape of employment and, 3–5
    competitive integrated employment of, 67–68
    identifying their own employment goals, 32
    improving skills in, 113
    living in small towns/rural areas, 115–116
    not wanting to work, 114–115
    overcoming inappropriate behavior in, 113–114
    overcoming poor hygiene in, 109–110
    overcoming severe disabilities in, 112–113
    overcoming unrealistic goals in, 110–111
    as ready and reliable employees, 30–33
    self-advocacy by, 33
    self-determination by, 24, 31, 33
    as self-employed, 45
    statistics on employment of, 2–3
    training and supports for (*see* training
        and supports)
    transportation for, 111
    work-based learning or internships for
        (*see* internships)
    see also employment of persons with disabilities
Plan for Achieving Self-Support (PASS), 42
Planning for employment, 27–28
    adult services agencies and, 42–43
    benefits planning in, 42
    deciding on employment options in, 43–46
    Employment First in, 33–34
    importance of, 29–30, 30*f*
    person-centered planning in (*see* person-centered
        planning)
    as ready and reliable employees, 30–33
Poor hygiene, 109–110
Poppin Joe's Kettle Korn, 45
Positive personal profile, 39*f*
Postschool indicators, 48
Postsecondary education areas of interest, 63
Pre-Employment Transition Services (Pre-ETS), 29,
        41, 45
Pre-ETS, *see* Pre-Employment Transition Services
Preparing students for employment, 77–79
Probationary time, job, 30–31
Project Skills, 61
Proposals, employment, 77, 78

Questions to ask supported employment providers, 44*f*

Rath, Tom, 118
Ready and reliable employees, 30–33
Realistic (concept), 31–33
Rehabilitation engineering, 99
Responding to work-related and social issues, 101–102
Retention, job, 102–105
Riehle, Erin, 61
Role playing by students, 18–19
Rural areas, limited opportunities in, 115–116

School experience, 47–48
    developing high school services for, 48–51
    establishing employment or postsecondary education
        areas of interest in, 63–65
    identifying learning styles and preferences in,
        51–54
    providing community work and internship
        opportunities, 61–63
    utilizing online career exploration tools in, 54
Self-advocacy, 33, 110
Self-determination, 24, 31, 33
    teaching, 92–93
Self-Directed Futures Curriculum, 54
Self-doubt, 118
Self-efficacy, 17
Self-employment, 45
Self-reflection, 110
Severe disability as barrier to employment, 112–113
Shared measurement system, 24
Situational assessments, 52, 54
    consumer, 55f–59f
    observational form, 60f
Skills, improvement of, 102, 113
    see also school experience
Small towns/rural areas, limited opportunities in,
    115–116
Social and guided activity, learning as, 21, 22b
Social issues, responding to, 101–102
Social Security Administration, 42
Social Security Disability Income (SSDI), 42
Social Security Red Book, 42
Social skills, 101–102
SSDI, see Social Security Disability Income
SSI, see Supplemental Security Income
Stanford Social Innovation Review, 9
Steffy, Joe, 45
StrengthsFinder, 118
Supplemental Security Income (SSI), 42
Supports
    instructional, 93–95
    natural, 95–105
    ongoing, plan form for, 104f
Systematic instruction, 95

Taking real action, 13
Task analysis, 93–95, 94f
Teachers, challenges faced by
    big job, 117
    learned passivity, 117–118
    momentum, 118
    self-doubt, 118
Teaching self-determination, 92–93
Technology, assistive, 98
Think aloud strategy, 18
Training and supports, 91–92
    assistive technology, 98
    compensatory strategies, 100
    employer negotiations, 101
    environmental modifications, 98–100
    identifying strategies for, 93
    implementing provisions for job retention in, 102–105
    instructional strategies in, 93–95
    natural supports, 95–105
    orientation, 83
    responding to work-related and social issues, 101–102
    teaching self-determination, 92–93
Transition to employment, 1–2
    collective impact in, 10–17
    Common Core State Standards and, 43
    crucial importance of collaboration in, 8–10
    as extended process, 7
    integrating best practices in, 17–25
    putting all pieces together in, 119
    see also planning for employment; training and supports
Transportation problems, 111

Universal Design for Learning (UDL), 17, 22
Unprepared students, 113–114
Unrealistic goals, 110–111

Vocational rehabilitation agencies, 3–4

WIOA, see Workforce Innovation & Opportunity Act
WIPA, see Work Incentive Planning and Assistance
    program
Work Incentive Planning and Assistance program, 42
Work opportunities, community, 61–63, 111
    reframing a perceived lack of, 116–117
    in small towns/rural areas, 115–116
Work-based learning, see internships
Workforce Innovation & Opportunity Act (WIOA)
    (PL 113-128), 3–4, 29, 67–68
Work-related behaviors, 101–102
Work-related issues, responding to, 101–102
Worksite analysis, 80, 82f